change agents

Also by Steve Chalke

Intelligent Church (Steve Chalke and Anthony Watkiss)

The Lost Message of Jesus (Steve Chalke and Alan Mann)

change agents:

25 hard-learned lessons
in the art of getting things done

steve chalke

ZONDERVAN®

ZONDERVAN.com/
AUTHORTRACKER
follow your favorite authors

Change Agents
Copyright © 2007 by Steve Chalke

Requests for information should be addressed to:

Zondervan, *Grand Rapids, Michigan 49530*

Library of Congress Cataloging-in-Publication Data

Chalke, Steve.
    Change agents : 25 hard-learned lessons in the art of getting things done /
Steve Chalke.
      p. cm.
   ISBN-13: 978-0-310-27549-7
   ISBN-10: 0-310-27549-0
   1. Change – Religious aspects – Christianity. 2. Entrepreneurship. 3. City
churches. 4. Christian communities. I. Title.
   BV4509.5.C425 2007
   253 – dc22
                                                  2007016778

Interior design by Mark Sheeres

Edited by Amy Lewis

Printed in the United States of America

08 09 10 11 12 • 12 11 10 9 8 7 6 5 4 3 2

contents

acknowledgements

A huge thank you to all my wonderful friends at Oasis, Faith-works and Church.co.uk; you have allowed me to write honestly about the joys and struggles of our life together, and I am indebted to you. Extra gratitude to Anthony Watkis, Ro Leech, Judith Doel, Steve Parker, Dan Nolloth, Dave Parr and Simon Chorley; you have all contributed beyond the call of duty to the production of this book. Also appreciation to John Buckeridge and Andy Peck, at *Christianity* magazine; you originally gave me the opportunity to write this material and have constantly encouraged me to keep going – respect.

introduction

Bill Bryson, in his book *A Short History of Nearly Everything*, quotes physicist Leo Szilard who once announced to his friend Hans Bethe that he was thinking of keeping a diary: 'I don't intend to publish. I am merely going to record the facts for the information of God.'

'Don't you think God knows the facts?' Bethe asked.

'Yes,' said Szilard. 'He knows the facts, but he does not know this version of the facts.'

Being a 'Change Agent' – a pioneer, an entrepreneur, an innovator, a leader within any charity, voluntary sector initiative, church or project – is a demanding task; I know. Since I founded the Oasis Trust in 1985, I have nursed and cared for it as it has grown through countless ups and downs, challenges and crises – through its infancy when I was the only member of staff, into childhood as a small team began to grow around me, during adolescence as we diversified both in terms of geography and areas of work and influence, and now in early adult life working in a growing number of countries around the world delivering housing, healthcare, education, training and employment in some of the poorest communities in the UK and around the world. In this process, not only has *it* developed and matured (though admittedly far too slowly and sometimes quite painfully), I have as well.

> 'I am merely going to record the facts for the information of God.'
> – Leo Szilard

People always told me I should keep a diary of the highs and lows, the perils and pleasures, the joys and sorrows of this journey – I have not done so and I've always regretted it. So in 2003, when as part of my role within Oasis, I became the minister of an old, struggling church in central London called Christ Church & Upton Chapel, I decided not to make the same mistake again and made the commitment to keep a journal of my experiences, good and bad. It was to be a kind of record from the frontline: an open and honest, first-hand, passionate, raw account of the joys and frustrations of church leadership and of the lessons that I learned, relearned or not learned, as the case may be. It is this journal that I have used as the raw material from which the twenty-five lessons in leadership this book contains have been formed.

Becoming the leader/minister/pioneer of a dying inner-city church is very demanding indeed. In the first eighteen months or so I'm sure I aged ten years – a view my barber unknowingly confirmed when he innocently enquired if I would like my hair 'dyed to a slightly younger colour?' He went on to assure me that, as I had gone grey so quickly, I could 'easily get away with it – no worries!' But that's exactly the problem. There were many long weeks and months – especially, as you may be able to detect from some of my earlier entries, during the first years – when I felt as though I were drowning in a sea of worries. I don't want to appear overly negative. The highs have been extremely high; it's just that some of the lows have been sub-zero. One moment you are up – the next you're overwhelmed again by a tide of paralysing criticism and, even worse, self-doubt. I've experienced great breakthroughs and triumphs, but I have also had to weather the storms of opposition and setback. One moment I'm celebrating, the next I'm reeling from letdown and disappointment. It's a roller-coaster ride. I once heard someone say, 'Being a parent is part joy, part guerrilla warfare.' Ditto that for both charity and church leadership.

So what is it that we are trying to achieve here at Church.
co.uk? Our goal is simple: To build a 'can-do' environment in
which we develop a model of church that demonstrates God's
love tangibly through providing the kind of 360-degree, wrap-
around care, nothing less than which can truly be known as the
gospel of Jesus Christ. We aim to be open twenty-four-hours a
day to offer holistic care to our local community. It may sound
strange, but what we aspire to is to become a kind of modern
Christian equivalent of a first-century synagogue.

The first Christians inherited their model of church from
their Jewish roots and, therefore, from their understanding of
the role of the local synagogue. Indeed, the first churches, like
the one in Jerusalem, could actually be better termed Mes-
sianic synagogues. The disciples simply believed that in Jesus
the Messiah had come, and they worshipped him within their
traditional culture. We tend to think of
synagogues of the New Testament
era as the Jewish equivalent of our
modern-day churches – buildings
to gather in on the Sabbath for
your weekly dose of 'word and
worship' and perhaps a mid-
week Bible study. But the truth is
that though synagogues did hold
Sabbath day services, their function was far broader and more central
to the whole of Jewish life than that. Not only
were synagogues the place of singing, sermons, prayers and
Bible readings, they also served as the entertainment centre, the school and lifelong learning centre, the welfare centre, the medical centre, the social centre and the town hall. In
short, the synagogue was the community hub, providing well
being (or as the ancient Jews would have put it, 'shalom' – the
presence of God's wholeness or completeness), meeting the

> What
> we aspire
> to is to become
> a kind of modern
> Christian equivalent
> of a first-century
> synagogue.

physical, emotional, educational, social and spiritual needs of the entire community.

As it provides the context against which the lessons in leadership and change management contained in this book are written, it's also essential to give you a brief overview of the history of Church.co.uk.

Christ Church & Upton Chapel (which, as you will discover during the course of this book, became known as Church.co.uk in the spring of 2005) has a truly remarkable past. On 8 June 1783, it began its life under the leadership of Roland Hill, a close friend of George Whitfield and a well-known figure in London. At this stage it was known as Surrey Chapel (don't ask!). During the following years, it was to become a major influence in the birth of the Bible Society, the Ragged School Movement and several other significant Christian initiatives. Ragged Schools were established long before any formal state education system was in place. Before the Elementary Education Act of 1870, the Church in the UK was all but the sole provider of schooling. Surrey Chapel was responsible for developing a dozen or so schools.

During the late 1700s and early years of the next century, William Wilberforce and friends made Surrey Chapel a central London base. Many of their antislavery meetings and debates took place there as the church became a community of spiritual vision and political engagement for countless people. Its new building, known as Christ Church, was opened in July 1876 on Westminster Bridge Road in the heart of London. The tower was donated by Abraham Lincoln's family and friends to thank the church for their inspiration and support in the battle for the emancipation of the slaves in America.

By 1900 Christ Church had a regular Sunday morning congregation of around 2,500 people. Nicknamed 'The Nonconformist Cathedral', these were the days of its greatest and widest influence. For instance it set up a whole football league (indeed, as is well known, many of England's present day Premiership clubs were born out of the work of local churches). One of its long-term members and leaders – George Williams – became the founder of the YMCA. Christ Church also developed a number of almshouses to provide housing for the poor and elderly, and it functioned as a substantial healthcare provider for the poor. From the official records for 1900 we know that the church's medical staff carried out eleven major operations, twenty-four minor operations and delivered fifty-six babies in that year alone.

> The Church chose to sit rehearsing its doctrines and passing the time by singing its songs to itself.

But troubled times were ahead. Tragically, during the Blitz, at the beginning of World War II, on 10 September 1940, the Christ Church building was almost totally destroyed by a German bomb. Only the Lincoln tower survived. Within days, Upton Chapel, a nearby Baptist church building (Christ Church had always been independent of any denomination), was also bombed. As a result, the two congregations began to work together. In fact, in 1943 they reached the decision to form a united fellowship – Christ Church & Upton Chapel.

At the same time British social policy was changing. Many of the roles that the church in the UK had traditionally taken responsibility for – education, healthcare, the care of the elderly – were increasingly taken over by the state. In 1948 the National Health Service (NHS) was born. The idea was revolutionary – free and accessible healthcare for all. Indeed, even today the World Health Organisation still recognise the NHS as one of the best health services in the world. State provision of healthcare, like education some years before, did much to reduce inequality and raised the overall standard of living in the UK. The Church, however, found itself stripped of a major role it had played within society for generations. This simply accelerated and exacerbated an already apparent trend – the great move indoors. Instead of innovation, the Church's response was retreat. Instead of the bold societal involvement that in previous generations had produced the likes of Wilberforce, Shaftsbury, the Booths and Florence Nightingale, the Church chose to sit rehearsing its doctrines and passing the time by singing its songs to itself. The level of debate was reduced to such incidentals as refurbishing the kitchen and the colour of cups.

So it was that on Pentecost Sunday, 8 June 2003, exactly 220 years to the day after Surrey Chapel's founding, Christ Church & Upton Chapel asked Oasis Trust to work with it. I found myself the minister of a church that was a mere shadow of its former self. Not only had its membership fallen from over two thousand in the early years of the 1900s to less than twenty, but even the memory of the medical, the educational or the sports teams who had once been based here as part of the church's holistic, 360-degree, wrap-around-care approach had been long forgotten. Indeed, on my first day I was given a copy of the membership list only to discover that, of the few names remaining, a fair percentage had absolutely no connection with the church any more. A great institution of London life had become a tiny huddle of people, meeting for a single hour each week in a giant building. And, both extremely exciting and deeply worrying, I was responsible for its future – either its final hour or its renewal through the discovery of a Christ-centred vision for the twenty-first century.

No external transformation without internal transformation.

It was time to re-image not just the shape of church but also the scope of its mission and purpose. I believe that where we rise to this challenge, local churches could, once again, become the hubs of their communities. Even from government there is a new tone. For, if the church found itself redundant as the State took more and more responsibility for the provision of welfare, the government increasingly found itself overstretched and under-resourced. The loss of voluntary support on such a massive scale has had, over time, a devastating impact on the life of our local communities and society as a whole. As a result, present political thinking is doing all it can to stimulate and encourage what it calls the 'voluntary sector' (that's us!) to re-engage in working in partnership alongside statutory agencies (healthcare, education, youth services, police, social services, and so on) to achieve change and build healthy communities. On top of all this, there is also an increasing openness to understanding that spiritual health is a vital ingredient for everyone's overall well-being. In the end you can't achieve community change without individual change – no external transformation without internal transformation.

> We need a new generation of Nightingales and Wilberforces who will redefine Christian service in the twenty-first century.... I call these people 'Change Agents'.

It is my belief that we need a new generation of Nightingales and Wilberforces who will redefine Christian service in the twenty-first century. We need men and women who, because of their commitment to Christ, can't help but help people; a new crop of social entrepreneurs who will take the skills of business and actively invest them in the building of the kingdom of God; a new army that is prepared to fight need, whatever its form, wherever it is encountered in Christ's name; a new leadership that rather than being content to tell tales of an impressive past, seeks to forge an innovative future. I call these people 'Change Agents' and this book is for them. I hope this book is for you.

change agents

One last point of introduction: to protect the wonderful people with whom I work and worship, names have been changed and occasionally people, events and circumstances have been fused together to form the stories I tell. That is to say, my promise is that everything you read in *Change Agents* is absolutely true – but not all of it happened in exactly the form presented here.

others only ever see your mountaintop experiences

Tim is a friend of mine who leads a church on the other side of London. Yesterday morning he came to meet with me in our coffee shop – The Hub. We chatted over lattes about life, our families and church. He asked me how we set up The Hub (which is kind of 'Starbucks' in style) so I explained. I was just going to offer to buy him another drink when suddenly he blurted out in a rather aggressive tone, 'It's easy for you; you've got it all on a plate. You were just born ...' I knew how he wanted to end his short sentence: 'You were just born ... lucky.' The problem was that being both a convinced Christian and a card-carrying Calvinist, he had a problem. In his world the only legitimate words with which he could conclude his sentence were 'chosen', 'elect' or 'anointed,' and he didn't want to go there!

Whatever dilemmas Tim's outburst caused for his theology, it did wonders for the honesty of our conversation. And as we talked, I realised that, because of the vulnerability and pain of his own situation, Tim had come to resent not only me, but any success that any other leader enjoyed. Jesus may have taught us to 'weep with those who weep and rejoice with those who rejoice', but Tim's struggle had led him to develop a flair for weeping and

'It's easy for you...
You were just
born lucky'
– Tim

17

gnashing his teeth over the success of others while secretly smirking over their failures and shortcomings.

Twenty-four hours after my encounter with Tim I was still reflecting on what he said. Does he honestly think that my life is anymore plain sailing than his? Does he imagine that I don't experience the bad days, weeks, months and indeed whole years where, like everyone else, I just have to put my head down and struggle through?

But if I'm really honest, the most disturbing part of my conversation with Tim was that I could see so much of myself in him. What is it about me that is so ready to assume the other guy has got it easier than me? That if someone else has made any progress or achieved a goal it must be a fluke, a mistake or because the cards were somehow stacked unfairly in their favour.

I realise, as a wise friend told me years ago, 'Other people only see your Mountaintop Experiences.' They don't witness the hours you spend lying awake, desperate to sleep, trying to plan a route out of what feels like 'the valley of the shadow of death'. They don't know how often you think about giving up altogether.

We opened The Hub café in the foyer of our church building as part of our efforts to fulfil one of our goals – becoming a 24/7 'hub' for the local community. The problem is that Tim only saw a smart coffee shop with comfortable seating and a welcoming ambiance, not the months of unsociable hours and constant frustrating setbacks that it took to get it off the ground. Tim sees the mochas in trendy cups, not the mind-numbing debate over why the church should 'want to run a coffee shop instead of preaching the gospel', the subsequent battle to raise funding, the fight to get a licence from the local council, the perpetual question of why prayer is sometimes answered and yet sometimes seems to go completely unheard. He didn't feel the pain of the patience-sapping conversations and negotiations that ate up my life evening after evening when all I really wanted to do was go home.

Talking with Tim reminded me of a conversation I'd had with a member of our original congregation in the coffee shop. I asked her if she liked the fact that the church building was open for more of the time (a year ago we only did one hour a week!). She sipped her cappuccino and didn't reply immediately. She informed me that she was disappointed 'we don't do sandwiches'. It was, by coincidence, the exact moment where if I'd had a sandwich handy I'd have shoved it straight down her throat. Why can't people celebrate the progress that has been made? Why don't they recognise how much work goes into even the tiniest achievement? Over these last months I'm learning again how hard it is just to stand still, let alone make any progress!

> I'm learning again how hard it is just to stand still, let alone make any progress!

Other people, looking in from the outside, will always see my so-called successes, viewing them from a superficial vantage point. What they will never see are the hundreds of failed ideas and abandoned dreams that have consumed just as much, if not more, of my time and energy (physically, spiritually and emotionally).

Looking back, I don't blame Tim for thinking my life is easy – he only gets to see my Mountaintop Experiences. Why would he ever suspect that each one is the result of a long hard climb out of a pretty deep valley and is enjoyed only for a moment or two before the next descent begins?

But then again, I suppose I would like him to learn, for his own sake, that most of my life, just like his, is spent struggling over some pretty uninviting, rugged, uphill terrain – often climbing alone. To change the metaphor for a moment, church leadership has, as they say of Wagner's music, 'some wonder-ful moments but some very long half hours!' Or, to come back to where we started, others only ever see your Mountaintop Experiences.

respond, don't react

They say when you arrive at a church as a new minister you get a 'honeymoon period' – the calm before the storm. My honeymoon period is, I'm sorry to say, well and truly over. In fact if I'm honest, it was over almost before it began. It turned out to be no longer than my actual honeymoon: two weeks.

In one of our church meetings, a member stood up to point out that I show no signs of being a leader and asked whether I had any kind of certificate to prove my credentials.

If, as my wife occasionally suggests, I am actually married to the church, we are now into the domestic equivalent of trying to cope with toddler tantrums and frequent food slinging. Looking back I really should have seen it coming. At my induction/commissioning service I was handed the keys to the door of the church building – it was a symbolic and ceremonious act, but it also turned out to be prophetic. The very next day, when I went to use them for the first time, I promptly gashed my finger on a piece of jagged metal sticking out from the door. It's now one-and-a-half-years later and I've still got that scar.

> I have to confess that I find church meetings to be some of the darkest hours of my life.

Our church, being an amalgamation of two congregations, is affiliated to both the Baptist and United Reformed denominations. As part of this arrangement we have inherited what they call 'the rich tradition of the church meeting'. Under this time-honoured system the leaders of a local congregation are regularly given the opportunity to present the ideas, plans and strategies that they have thought about, prayed through, agonised over, costed and debated to the rest of the church community only to have them ridiculed, rubbished and rejected. Unfortunately, in my experience, many of the normally lovely people in the churches that I have worked in over the last twenty-five years, undergo some sort of werewolf-like change in nature as they enter these church meetings. Though in real life they are wonderful, generous and responsible, here they are transformed – they instantly become hypercritical, argumentative, obstinate and often illogical as they proceed to metaphorically 'beat their ploughshares into swords' and wave them furiously at one another. I have to confess that I find church meetings to be some of the darkest hours of my life – and I'm pretty sure I'm not alone. But then I remember the words of Churchill: 'Democracy is the worst form of government – except for all the others!'

I don't want to sound in any way negative about the life of our church – these last years have been some of the most exciting I can remember. We are a good team, we have fun, we've grown by a factor of five and have started to get some genuinely innovative community projects off the ground. But, that said, it has also been a time of stress, worry and anxiety. I've felt under massive pressure, and I know that other people have suffered as a result. My comments and observations at church meetings haven't always exhibited the patience and understanding that people need and deserve. Change is essential but it often hurts. My conversation and attitude (not to mention diary) after meetings has sometimes been grumpy, jumpy and occasionally down right rude. And I know that there have been occasions when I've been so worried that people were going to have another go at me that I've ended up reacting badly and going for the 'pre-emptive strike' instead of listening to what they had to say with an open mind.

Recently I read a book about management styles that suggested 'ego strength' is a key to building healthy relationships. It's a strange term and I'm not sure I like it, but I haven't been able to get the idea out of my head ever since. It takes a great deal of personal strength to listen to other people (who often misunderstand or misrepresent you and your ideas) without constantly trying to jump in and defend yourself. I remember one of my mentors years ago teaching me to 'let others go first' – to have the strength of character to listen and reflect, knowing that my moment to speak will come and I don't have to force it. Having the confidence to wait, rather than jumping into the fray with guns blazing, and then to speak graciously is a hallmark of great maturity. Ambrose Bierce summed it up when he wrote, 'Speak when you are angry and you will make the best speech you will ever regret.' I've made a few of those!

'Speak when you are angry and you will make the best speech you will ever regret' – Ambrose Bierce

From now on I am determined to do all that I can to respond rather than react – which probably means, amongst other things, sitting through our next church meeting with a slightly more gracious attitude.

you can't be everyone's best mate

Here's a secret – I don't like it when people don't like me. I want people to think I'm a good guy. When they don't, it hurts. To be honest, I think that even if my skin were as thick as a rhino's, I still wouldn't be able to withstand some of the negative comments I receive unscathed. I don't believe those experts who say that you need ten positive comments to cancel out each negative one – I think it must be at least fifty!

> Leadership is about taking a lead and making decisions, which means that tension, and sometimes even conflict, is inevitable.

It was one of those weeks. On Sunday morning I was attacked for the way I led communion: 'It's not like it used to be, and we don't like it', I was forcefully told. Then I was criticised about the people who smoke before the service on the church steps – 'People never used to do things like that. It sends the wrong messages.' My secret response, under my breath, was – because of the way the communion service was done, no one ever used to stand on the church steps to do anything!

It was when I worked as a minister in the early '80s at Tonbridge Baptist Church in Kent, that I found myself plunged, for the first time, into a sea of self-doubt created by the impossible struggle to fulfil other people's expectations of me. In the middle of it all a good friend told me that one of my biggest problems was that I always wanted everyone to like me. 'Get over it' he barked at me. 'Mark my words, if you don't you will never achieve anything.' A week later he followed up this sensitive comment by sending me a postcard. The caption read, 'If you don't like the heat get out of the kitchen.' It wasn't exactly the encouragement I was looking for – but his advice was true then and remains true to this day. Leadership is about taking a lead and making decisions, which means that tension, and sometimes even conflict, is inevitable.

Speaking of postcards brings another one to mind – the one I used to have blu-tacked to the fridge. It features a cartoon illustration of Moses parting the Red Sea. Behind him stand a small group of Israelites looking out from the shore at the water miraculously rising up in two giant walls either side of a puddled pathway stretching into the distance. The only speech bubble comes from the mouth of one of the reluctant looking Israelites who is complaining to Moses 'You never said it would be muddy!'

It's one of the greatest challenges of leadership. You can't lead anyone anywhere unless you are prepared to make decisions that make you unpopular with some of the people some of the time (not to mention a few of them just about all of the time). Jesus might have claimed, 'The truth will set you free' (John 8:32), but he never suggested it wouldn't hurt first.

'You just can't be a public servant and be everyone's best mate.'

I couldn't get those comments about communion and smoking on the church steps out of my head. I found myself endlessly replaying them again. Then I remembered a conversation I had a year or so ago with a friend of mine who is a Member of Parliament. She was talking about how often members of her constituency complain, 'You just don't listen to us.' She made the point that, in fact, an MP listens to many more people than most. 'The average person', she said, 'probably only has a fairly small circle of friends in terms of those that they actually consult. And most of them share the same basic views, attitudes and outlook, which is why they are friends in the first place. On the other hand, an MP's job, as a public servant, is to spend their whole life listening to as wide a variety of people as possible.... But', she added with a smile, 'listening to someone isn't necessarily the same thing as agreeing with them. What most people mean when they say, "You don't listen to me," is actually, "You don't do what I tell you to".' She concluded, 'You just can't be a public servant and be everyone's best mate.'

I feel the same. I listen to loads of people who hold a wide spectrum of opinions on just about everything from how to celebrate communion to what makes a good hymn and smoking on the church steps to the spiritual state of women who wear clothing that exposes their midriffs. That's part of my job. Unfortunately when I stop long enough to listen to so many opinions, it is impossible to agree with them all and inevitably I will be criticised.

So here's what I decided: we will do communion differently! And we will not be offended when people smoke on the church steps – in fact we will be glad that they are part of our community! Not because I'm not listening but because I am listening hard and using my best judgement to make the wisest decisions I can. But I know that however good my decisions are – because they *are* decisions – I'll never be everyone's best mate.

every 'yes' implies at least one 'no'

The experts say that 'the first 500 years in any institution's history are always the most difficult'. And they are right!

We've finally made a momentous decision about what has been a contentious issue: we've changed the name of our church, though not for the first time in its history. Over the years it's been variously known as Surrey Chapel, Green Walk Chapel, Upton Chapel, Christ Church, Christ Church & Upton Chapel and most recently by the abbreviation Christ Church & Upton. From 26 January 2005, however, our name is officially 'Church. co.uk, Waterloo'.

Why did we do it? Well, first, Christ Church & Upton Chapel is two names, not one. Second, neither of them tells you where we actually are! People regularly ring our office to enquire about Christ Church in Upton – 'I just can't find you on the map; is Upton anywhere near Streatham?'

Although the problems created by our former name have been clear to all, the arguments about what to change it to and whether to change it at all, have been complex, time consuming and contro-versial. There weren't any easy answers, but diagnosing the problem is always simpler than finding a solution. Or,

Diagnosing the problem is always simpler than finding a solution.

29

change agents

put another way, being in opposition is a lot easier than being in government.

All of that aside, we formally agreed that from now on, we are 'Church.co.uk, Waterloo' – a name that lets you know where to find us on the World Wide Web as well as in London – and I am happy.

I feel like the man who has just walked a thousand miles against the wind and finally made it to his destination – a place of rest and celebration. I like to think that I'm an averagely pastoral sort of guy, which means that my natural inclination is to expend a great deal of energy and time trying to avoid the dreaded 'c' word – *conflict*. I've lived the last twenty-five years, however, with a deep and unresolved tension because I also understand three truths: leadership is about leading somewhere; leading inevitably involves dealing with disagreement; and (this is the most uncomfortable one of all) you can't say yes to everything because almost every 'yes' implies at least one 'no', probably more.

If I'm honest, in the back of my mind there is still a nagging fear that there could be trouble ahead – will the renaming of the church lead to mutiny or some sort of attempted coup d'état? Mind you I've already heard every possible argument on either side, so I think I'm ready for whatever comes my way.

'Church.co.uk. It's not churchy enough', some have complained. 'We should call ourselves "Christ Church, Waterloo" or "Waterloo Baptist Church" or "Oasis Community Church". "Church.co.uk" is far too flippant.'

'Church.co.uk. It's far too churchy', others retort. 'The name "church" is a huge turn off – drop it altogether. We should be doing something new; something more creative like "Epiphany" or "Harvest" or simply the "Waterloo Community Centre". "Church.co.uk" is far too religious.'

'Church.co.uk is a Web address, not a name for a community – it will never catch on', some have argued. 'A Web address may be a clever idea for now, but it won't last. It's far too faddish', others have warned.

I know that leadership is intrinsically about journeying – about leaving the familiar behind and heading into the unknown. But I've realised again just how scary it is. In fact, it's a perfect incubation unit for insecurity. Have I made the right decision? What if I'm wrong? Even though the overwhelming majority of the membership voted for my suggestion, if the chips are down and it doesn't work it's my credibility on the line.

So in my insecurity I desperately tried to remind myself that unless leaders are leading somewhere they are just kidding themselves; that, though making a decision about moving forward is difficult, the worst decision is no decision; and that when leaders are indecisive both they and their people are almost guaranteed to become victims of the future rather than architects of it.

'Make no small plans; they do not move the hearts of men' – Daniel Burnham

I read a quote from Daniel Burnham: 'Make no small plans; they do not move the hearts of men.' Well, we made our plans and announced our intention. Only time will tell if we have chosen the right direction.

people matter more than programmes

'One volunteer', according to the old English proverb, 'is worth two pressed men.' If that's true, why do I find leading this church, which is filled with volunteers, and so many of the Oasis projects that are dependent on volunteers, so demanding and difficult?

If you wander around the building at Church.co.uk you'll discover various lists and sign-up sheets neatly pinned to a number of strategically placed notice boards. These indicate, to the casual observer, an air of calm efficiency. But this impressive façade masks a hidden truth – the appearance of any name on any rota (welcome, coffee, sound desk, etc.) is often almost totally unrelated to whether or not anything will happen as a result.

> 'One volunteer
> is worth two
> pressed men'
> – English proverb

'Leave it to me ...' 'Trust me ... I'll sort it for you ...' 'Rely on me ... I'll do it ...' Though all of these terms are in common usage, none of them seems to bear any particular relation to whether or not the volunteer using them will actually deliver. If I am honest, half the time the problem is mine. I've attended countless seminars and workshops on people management. I've read a lorry load of books on the subject. And, here's the twist, I've even written one! It's called *Making a Team Work*. Oh, the deep irony! As they say, those who can, do – those who can't, teach.

I remember once, in my frustration over exactly this kind of issue, I rang a friend of mine to vent my spleen. I concluded the five-minute tirade of ungraciousness that I inflicted on him with, what was at that moment, a heartfelt piece of wisdom: 'Never ever work with animals, children or volunteers!' But his response gave me loads to think about. I had been hoping it would – I guess that's why I rang him in the first place. He told me a story about a couple in his church who helped lead the kids' work every Sunday morning. They were extremely reliable and dedicated, until right out of the blue, they took to not turning up occasionally – no phone call, no notice, no show! It happened once, then again several weeks later. After that the floodgates opened, and it began to look like a regular habit.

I asked my friend what he did about it. His response was that he eventually got so frustrated and angry that he sat down to give them a piece of his mind. 'It was only then', he told me, 'that I realised the problem was two-sided. Their problem was that they should have stuck to their commitment or, alternatively, taken the initiative to sit down with me to re-negotiate it.' Then he made his most telling observation, 'However, I realised that *we* had let them down badly. We didn't understand the nature of volunteering, the pressures on them in other areas of their life and the level of support that they needed from us to sustain their commitment over the long haul.'

That conversation reminded me of something I read a few years ago from Bill Hybels, the North American Church leader. He made the point that working with volunteers involves the purest form of leadership in the world. The reason, he said, is simple – employees will often endure bad leadership,

Never ever work with animals, children or volunteers!

put up with a lack of stimulation or cope with deep dissatisfaction for the money. A good pay packet covers over a multitude of sins. But for volunteers no such monetary incentive exists. If their work is not fulfilling, they will vote with their feet.

Working with volunteers may be demanding, but across the life of Church.co.uk the number of hours and the amount of expertise they contribute each and every week is huge. And, of course, that they *are* Church.co.uk! They are wonderful, talented, keen to serve, but struggle, just like me, to juggle all the responsibilities of life. That means they deserve clear and realistic boundaries, consistent support, good communication and regular encouragement in their work. My problem is that I can get so absorbed with my fascination for setting goals and measuring outcomes that I forget project management is not the same thing as people management.

> Jesus ... never pushed, forced, bludgeoned, beat, coerced, cajoled, manhandled or manipulated people.... Instead he inspired them.

Reading a section of John's gospel I realised again that the extraordinary thing about Jesus is that he never pushed, forced, bludgeoned, beat, coerced, cajoled, manhandled or manipulated people. He never bullied them into submission; instead he inspired them. As John Donne, the seventeenth-century Anglican poet and preacher, put it, 'Christ beats his drum, but he does not press men; Christ is served with volunteers.'

He was right! I know that the management technique of nagging never works anyway. Or, put another way, in the words of Walter Brueggemann, 'People [*volunteers*] are not changed by moral exhortation but by transformed imagination.'

action leads to insight more often than insight leads to action

To misquote Charles Dickens ever so slightly, 'This is the best of times, this is the worst of times.' A couple of months ago we decided to extend the opening hours of The Hub Café, our very successful coffee shop, by staying open late every Wednesday evening. We envisaged throngs of people relaxing at the end of the day, sampling our excellent coffees and enjoying animated conversation about life, the universe and everything. Wednesday evenings at The Hub were set to become the last word in spiritual as well as liquid refreshment. But it just didn't work – hardly anyone turned up. Last week we finally bit the bullet and abandoned the idea. Late-night opening is not for us – at least not yet.

The failure of The Hub's extended opening is just the latest in a growing list of initiatives we've attempted at Church.co.uk that haven't quite worked out. But for some unknown reason, this one has created a ferocious backlash. 'Was keeping The Hub open later a "God idea" or just a "good idea"?' I've been asked. 'Was it even a "good idea" or nothing more than a "Steve idea"?' someone else wanted to know. 'And if it wasn't a God idea, perhaps some of the other ideas you've introduced aren't God ideas either!'

'A "God idea" or just a "good idea"?'

they added. 'The problem with you', one person explained to me, in a pseudo-pastoral tone, yesterday morning, 'is that you've always got a new idea up your sleeve. But the question is', she ventured, taking on a strange, otherworldly air, 'can you truly say that the Lord is in them?'

All this has left me feeling like a second-rate, latter-day psalmist – 'My accusers circle round me like hungry vultures. Why have you humiliated me in the presence of the scoffers?'

Over the years I've learnt that when any idea I introduce doesn't work out, I will inevitably be accused of attempting to do the Lord's work 'in the flesh', of being impulsive and out of step with his will or timing, or both. Whenever an idea does work, however, I'll be hailed as a visionary, 'a real man of God' and naturally in tune with the Spirit. Of course I'm old enough to know that both assessments lack a little discernment, not to mention objectivity. Can we really claim that every idea a church or Christian project has put into action successfully has been a faithful reflection of God's will, or, on the other hand, dismiss all those that have failed as being out of line with his purpose?

When I first applied to train as a Baptist minister I was interviewed by a large committee whose responsibility it was to accept or reject me. I was just twenty at the time. I sat in a large hall on a stage, in front of forty or so middle-aged and elderly people, 95 percent of whom were male. They pummelled me with questions, and I did my best to answer. I was naïve and immature. I'm sure I would answer my torturers (sorry, 'questioners') differently, and hopefully, more wisely, today. I will, however, always remember one of the assembled group, charged with the task of weeding out the wheat from the chaff of prospective ministerial students, looking straight at me and barking, 'Young man, your problem is that you are an activist. And the last thing the Baptist ministry needs right now is any more activists.' I didn't know what to say. It seemed to me the very thing the Baptists needed more urgently than anything was activists – as many as possible! Shortly after my interview was over, I found myself waiting in an ancillary room until another member of this 'nonconformist conclave' arrived to explain to me that I had been 'declined a place'. I cried all the way home.

Reflecting again on the events and questions raised by the failure of our coffee shop experiment, I'm content that it was the right decision to try opening on Wednesday evenings. It didn't work out, but we learned an important lesson or two and gained some valuable experience. It's good to be an activist.

Dr. George Carey, the then Archbishop of the Church of England, tagged the '90s the 'Decade of Evangelism' for the Church in the UK. My prayer is that the first years of this third millennium will be remembered as a decade of experimentation. Why? Because progress is born of struggle – it is the child of pain, sweat, tears and lots of mistakes. In the words of an old African proverb, 'Smooth seas do not make skilled sailors.' Or, to put it differently, action, even when it ends in failure, leads to insight more often than insight leads to action.

> Progress is born of struggle – it is the child of pain, sweat, tears and lots of mistakes.

the journey with others is slower than the journey alone

It's very simple to be wise. Just think of something stupid to say and then don't say it! That's just my problem. In theory I've got it sorted. But as they say, 'In theory, practise is the same as theory. However, in practise, what's true in theory is hard to practise.'

So, as a result, I often feel like awarding myself an ASBO – an Anti-Social Behavioural Order. Why? For one, at a recent strategy meeting my attitude and approach owed more to the example of Genghis Kahn than Mother Teresa.

> At a recent strategy meeting my attitude and approach owed more to the example of Genghis Kahn than Mother Teresa.

The most irritating thing is that I was simply trying to get everyone else to see the road ahead and plot a new course for all of our benefit. I have endless weaknesses and failings, but one thing I can do is see the way ahead – I think I know where we need to be headed.

Let me qualify that last statement. First, I know I sometimes get it wrong. Second, I know that the growth of Church.co.uk is actually all down to God. We are dependent on him. Without him, we are finished – I don't doubt that for a nanosecond. However, it is also true that the Lord likes to work in partnership. That means, humanly speaking, had I not given a strong lead and set a clear direction over the last two years, we wouldn't have developed a viable church here to hold a strategy meeting about in the first place. Why can't people give me some credit, cut me a bit of slack, accept my advice and just get on with it?

A few weeks ago, in a very different context, I found myself sitting in a room with about twenty other people discussing a certain issue. Eventually we reached a conclusion that, to be blunt, many of us could have worked out in five minutes without any discussion at all. But as someone else in the room later wisely explained to me, 'It's the process that's important, we got there together and, as a result, everyone feels a sense of ownership.' It was a very good point. The journey with others is slower than the journey alone. It's the lesson from the old story of the 'Hare and the Tortoise' – it is not always the contestant that can run the fastest that reaches the destination first.

> 'You do not lead by hitting people over the head – that's assault, not leadership' – Dwight D. Eisenhower

Dwight D. Eisenhower once said, 'You do not lead by hitting people over the head – that's assault, not leadership.' I know he's right but, in my defence, at the strategy meeting I felt over-tired, overworked, overstretched, underloved, undervalued and, in consequence, in the mood to hit out. So I consoled myself that, as another slightly less ambitious, but perhaps more realistic, writer once put it, 'The man who first flung a word of abuse at his enemy instead of a punch was the founder of civilisation.'

I know that the mature, Christ-like thing to have done was to have kept my cool. The wise are conciliatory; the prudent stay composed; the shrewd remain calm; the discreet only make considered responses. But the trouble is that on the inside I got myself really wound up, and, as a result, though on the outside I didn't exactly explode, I couldn't stop myself from showing that I was irritated by getting a little bit too belligerent.

A Catholic priest who is a friend of mine says, 'In the midst of every growing church there is a dying priest.' In truth, of course, this is nothing more or less than the way of the cross. So why do I complain about it so vociferously? The curious truth is that I know the same people who sometimes seem to be doing all they can to frustrate me, will on a different night, be risk-taking, encouraging and supportive. I also know that I love working with them and, when in more balanced mood, enjoy the journey together, however long and winding the road we take may be.

'In the midst of every growing church there is a dying priest.'

under promise, over deliver

As a young boy my father taught me that 'magnificent promises are always to be suspected. A promise made is a debt unpaid.' Forty-years on I can still hear his challenge echoing around my head.

My problem is that I'm an enthusiast and sometimes my enthusiasm carries me away. Recently a friend introduced me as 'the man who has more ideas before breakfast than I've had in the last ten years'. A couple of thoughts came to me: one, he was being a bit hard on himself and two, I may have loads of ideas, but that doesn't mean that any of them are achievable. The fact that I can wax lyrical about them doesn't necessarily make them workable – it just makes people more susceptible to following me into oblivion if I've got it wrong.

All this reminds me of an important lesson that I learned a few years ago – one that I urgently need to brush up on. I was working as a presenter for a Breakfast TV channel when a huge earthquake hit India. Sixty-six villages in Maharashtra State were totally destroyed. More than 25,000 people lost their lives and 150,000 more were made homeless in just forty-three seconds.

I had an idea! I did some research and a few weeks later went to see

'Magnificent promises are always to be suspected.'

Peter, the director of programmes, to put to him a proposal. I suggested that he send me, along with a TV crew, out to Maharashtra and that we should launch a campaign to build a hospital there. I explained that other charities were already planning housing and schools, but no one as yet had stepped forward to handle the rebuilding of vital medical facilities. It was hard work convincing him, but eventually he and the other directors agreed and an appeal called 'Get Up and Give' was born.

There was just one sticking point, however. I wanted to launch a campaign to raise £1 million, but Peter disagreed. He said we should be more cautious. I said these people needed our help and that we should throw caution to the wind. He said that it was essential we built the confidence of our audience through our ability to deliver on what we promised. 'Go for a million if you like, but don't broadcast it because if you publicise a million and only collect £950,000 they will say that we failed. Whereas, if you come up with a more conservative estimate and then deliver more the campaign will be remembered as a huge success. The vital principle', he said, 'is "under promise and over deliver" – not the other way around.'

We did it his way (mainly because he was the boss and I had no choice) and though it hurts to say, he was right. I aimed (privately) at a million, but never told our audience. On air we said that our goal was to raise at least £500,000, which was honest although in my mind the words 'at least' were in big bold letters, double underlined in red. We budgeted building the hospital on £600,000 and eventually raised around £750,000. As a result our audience were happy – they raised a lot more than their target. The TV station's managers were happy because the campaign was a huge success – we even won a national award. The Indian health agency we were partnering with was happy because they got more money than they were expecting. I was happy because not only did we have enough to build the hospital, we were also able to pay all the staff costs for the first year. And to cap it all off, the appeal was such a success that the TV station adopted it for the next ten years and went on to raise another £7 million for many other charities.

It was there that I first learned the principle of under promising and over delivering, rather than what comes more naturally to me – wildly over promising and then dramatically under delivering. It's a lesson that is vitally important for everyone with an entrepreneurial spirit; every Change Agent. We are, by nature, people with big dreams, big visions, big

> It's what we do that counts, not what we say we'll do.

ideas and, more often than not, big mouths. Given even the remotest fragment of a chance to talk about our latest plans we will make grand promises of how our new project will change the world.

But when we 'talk up' our ideas too much we run the risk of setting such exaggerated goals that we can never hope to achieve them. The result, of course, is bound to be disappointment, distrust and eventually disillusionment. However, if we scale down our rhetoric (if not our ambitions), we give ourselves a fighting chance of exceeding people's expectations. In the end it is at the point of delivery that everyone is measured. It's what we do that counts, not what we say we'll do. To set expectations higher than we can ever hope to deliver, however well-meaning our excited talk, is to handicap our project and our people before we have even begun. Instead, look for targets that motivate rather than intimidate, goals that are achievable rather than unbelievable.

Machiavelli once wrote that, in his opinion, leaders should feel free to view 'the promise given as a necessity of the moment: the word broken as a necessity of tomorrow'. He was wrong. My dad was right: 'A promise made is a debt unpaid.'

nothing is ever quite as good or as bad as it first seems

lesson 9

I had trouble sleeping and, as a result, learned a valuable lesson: never download your emails last thing at night! Whatever you do, resist the thought that it is always best to be up-to-date with 'things'. However strong the temptation to go online just to make sure things are okay, fight it for all you are worth. Once you've given in and downloaded those little terrors, it's impossible to resist opening them, and that, as I discovered yesterday, is a recipe for deep despair.

The problem is that almost all the emails I ever get are about things that need doing, sorting, reviewing, solving, preparing, fixing, disputing, debating, defending or just plain stopping! At times it's down right depressing, but it's definitely never a formula for a good night's sleep – which is why I found myself, feeling besieged and utterly overwhelmed, still staring at my computer screen in the early hours of the morning. I can just about remember a line from doing Shakespeare at school that went something like, 'When sorrows come, they come not as single spies, but in battalions.' I think it's from *Hamlet*, but the point is – the Bard was dead right!

I kept trying to tell myself it was the middle of the night, I'd got things out of perspective and I'd feel a lot better in the morning – but it didn't help. My whole life felt like a desperate, futile failure. A pointless effort to fulfil the endless activities, responsibilities and commitments dumped on me by others (and there are hundreds of them that I've collected over the years) with no motivation left except duty.

I realised I was running on empty. I was totally isolated and felt that no one else could possibly understand what I was feeling or know what I was going through. In fact, I remember wondering who would care even if they did. Who would miss me if I was gone? Or would they all be secretly (or not so secretly) relieved? I didn't know what to do until it dawned on me – there was nothing I could do.

But of all those emails staring out at me from the screen, one of them hurt me far more than the rest put together. It was an outright attack on me. It cut like a knife and I still feel wounded by it. Why? Because it came from someone I have supported, nurtured, sacrificed for and given myself to over the years. Reading it through (which I did at least ten times) I felt like cruelty, spite, malice and injustice outweighed love and grace by a long way. I felt betrayed. But the terrible thing was that I could also feel my anger rising in return. On top of everything else – I was a hypocrite.

The worst thing of all was that I felt strangely separated from God. Desolate. My faith seemed to have instantly shredded. I couldn't think where to turn. Who could I ring in the middle of the night? I remember reading an article once about the connection between darkness and spiritual growth. If there is any connection between darkness and spiritual growth, it doesn't feel like it. It just hurts.

> I didn't know what to do until it dawned on me – there was nothing I could do.

M. Scott Peck said, 'The truth is that our finest moments are most likely to occur when we are feeling deeply uncomfortable, unhappy, or unfulfilled. For it is only in such moments, propelled by our discomfort, that we are likely to step out of our ruts and start searching for different ways or truer answers.' However, the more immediate question in the middle of the night is, will I be stuck like this forever? Will it feel like three in the morning, from now on, as I try to battle through all my regular day-to-day responsibilities?

> Many fears are born of fatigue, loneliness and of making the bad mistake of opening your emails last thing on a Friday night.

Trying to be as rational about it as I could, I remember thinking how I've slowly learnt over the years that even when I feel this way I'm generally able to keep functioning quite well 'on the outside' so that only those closest to me even begin to sense what I'm actually feeling 'on the inside'. But as successful as this is as a strategy for keeping going, it just makes the sense of isolation more intense.

With that night in the past, sitting here with a cup of coffee at 11.30 on Saturday morning and the sunlight gently spilling through my study window and caressing my desk, I have to admit that this morning the world feels very different.

They say that things always seem worse in the middle of the night. 'Many fears are born of fatigue and loneliness', wrote Max Ehrmann in his famous poem, 'Desiderata'. I'd like to update it: 'Many fears are born of fatigue, loneliness and of making the bad mistake of opening your emails last thing on a Friday night.'

This morning God doesn't seem so remote and there is hope. The issues haven't gone away, however. I've still got to deal with the same list of problems. My 'dark night' has passed. Nothing is ever quite as good or bad as it first seems. Now all I need is the courage to re-read those emails!

vision and frustration are the same thing

'Money is like manure; it's not worth a thing unless it's spread around encouraging young things to grow', said Thornton Wilder. That may be so but our church is broke. We are as poor as the proverbial church mouse, so just keeping things alive, let alone growing, is a challenge right now.

I'm greeted constantly by small mountains of requests for money from our various teams (youth, community development, pastoral care, children's, students', inclusion, prayer, music . . .), and I don't know what to do with any of them.

I try hard to be positive and focus on the upside of all this. The good news is that we've got a church full of entrepreneurs with an endless supply of great ideas – Change Agents with real plans to bring change to our local community. But the bad news is that we've got a church full of entrepreneurs with an endless supply of great ideas – that all need an endless supply of funding.

I hate being the person who has to say no, but I have no choice. I can almost feel people summing me up as 'the man with no vision'. The trouble with Change Agents is that they tend to be the kind of people whose favourite Bible verse is 'Ask and you will receive',

I hate being the person who has to say no.

which they appear to regard as a defining principle in their relationship with me as well as with the Almighty. But I often muse that if they enjoyed more success with this approach with him in the first place, then they wouldn't need to be quite so demanding of me.

Actually, if truth be told, the people who make up our church are very generous. Many of them give till it hurts. They give of their time and of their cash. Lots of them are poor, some of them are very poor indeed, and the needs around here are huge. In fact, that's just the problem: the more need we see, the more we do, but the more we do, the more need we see and the tougher it gets.

> Vision is longing for what is not yet; frustration is the inevitable result of longing for what is not yet.

I wish I could have a word with some of my old Sunday school teachers. When I was a kid I remember being reliably informed that 'God owns the cattle on a thousand hills' and that consequently 'the only thing that ever holds back his will is a lack of vision rather than money'. 'If the vision is there, the resources will always follow', they would regularly trumpet. Well, four decades later, I would like to venture the opinion that the only people who actually believe this are those who have no vision. It is indeed a load of old manure that's been spread around a bit!

I've learnt that to live with vision is to live with frustration. In fact, I've discovered that vision and frustration are the same thing. Vision is longing for what is not yet; frustration is the inevitable result of longing for what is not yet. You can't have one without the other.

I recently had a coffee with a friend of mine who is a Christian working in a high-powered, high-salaried job in the city. He told me that the previous weekend he heard a sermon on the theme of living by faith. But he went on to explain to me, he felt 'trapped' or 'boxed in'. Life, he said, is so structured and safe in our society that it leaves little room for real 'risk-taking' faith. He recounted that he had recently seen a quotation from Ralph Waldo Emerson that simply read, 'Money often costs too much.' He asked me to pray with him about how he could find a way of exercising greater faith. I did. But, as I prayed, I couldn't help thinking that my problem is almost the opposite of his. I wish that I could make it all the way to lunchtime, just occasionally, without facing some major hurdle of faith related to money.

I first became a church leader in 1981. Ever since then life has been a constant battle against a lack of resources – trying to be wise about the line between risk-taking faith and blind stupidity. I've spent more than a quarter of a century living this way. If money were as easy to get hold of as manure, I'd be the first to spread it around all over the place, because I know that if 'young things' aren't growing and being stretched they are stagnating at best and dying at worst. But I've also learnt that even though there is plenty of pressure to think otherwise, it is shallow to measure growth simply by the size of a budget, and that though it leaves me endlessly frustrated, the old proverb is right: it's 'without vision', not finance, 'that the people perish'!

success is three days between two crises

Good life balance is difficult to attain. I read an article by a 'spiritual life coach' about how to achieve it. The result was that I was left feeling that I am to 'the balanced life' what Mike Tyson is to ballet dancing.

The article in question was written by a church leader whose marriage is sublime, whose sex life is awe-inspiring, whose church is bigger than U2's fan club and runs more social welfare programmes than some world governments, whose prayer life makes those of Daniel, Shadrach, Meshach and Abednego look decidedly shallow, whose children have all inherited the spirit of Billy Graham, who reads more books in a month than I manage in a year and who still manages to work-out each day in order to 'honour God with his body' – not to mention keep in shape for the extraordinary demands of his sex life!

> I am to 'the balanced life' what Mike Tyson is to ballet dancing.

Once I'd had the opportunity to stop long enough to think about it, instead of being overwhelmed, I was angry. Not because I can't compete with this guy's output and track-record, but because I know he is being less than totally honest.

He is attempting to con me with yet another repackaging of the same old lies that only adds to the burden of so many good people already struggling to live in a way that honours God.

Earlier, rather appropriately as it turns out, I read the second half of Psalm 16. I've been aiming to read a Psalm a day for the last two months – and I've finally got to Psalm 16(b). It was written, so my Bible tells me, by King David. 'Therefore my heart is glad and my tongue rejoices … because you will not abandon me', his lyric boldly declares. The astonishing thing, as we all know, is that David – the king that God referred to as 'a man after his own heart' – was also a murderer, a liar and adulterer, not to mention a negligent and dysfunctional father. A few years ago, Bono wrote an introduction to the Psalms. In it he reflects on these incriminating facts. 'That the Scriptures are brim full of hustlers, murderers, cowards, adulterers and mercenaries used to shock me', he declares. 'Now it's a source of great comfort.'

I agree. Most of the time, if I'm honest, I'm just one or two steps away from the brink of total chaos. Successful living, for me, is three days between two crises. My life, just like everyone else's, is watermarked by stress and disorder. For me 'successful' living is really no more than the calm between inevitable storms. What frustrates me is that, from time to time, I still fall for the lie that life should be plain sailing, with nothing more than the occasional patch of rough sea. I still find myself momentarily falling for the belief that everyone else is on an even keel, and I'm the only one having trouble at the helm.

I remember when, soon after arriving at theological college, I confessed to my best friend that I was convinced I must be the most 'carnal' student ever accepted for ministerial training. Much of my time I lived in fear that my tutors would eventually discover the truth about me – bad on quiet times and spending far more time thinking about single women than spiritual warfare – and throw me out.

For me the picture of a squeaky-clean spirituality that enables one to climb any mountain and conquer any foe through the power of a disciplined prayer life is not just daunting, it's down-right dangerous. Over the years, I've seen too many Christian friends crash and burn because they've compounded the natural stress of their jobs with the myth that their lives are supposed to be constantly ordered, successful, triumphant and under control. The fact that they fall short simply adds another dimension to their already deep sense of failure and guilt. Overly high expectations, stress and burnout are huge problems for church leaders, pioneers and Change Agents –

> 'Success is the ability to go from one failure to another with no loss of enthusiasm' – Winston Churchill

physical exhaustion, illness, nervous exhaustion, breakdown, clinical depression, adultery, divorce, alcoholism, substance abuse, domestic violence, even suicide – I've witnessed all of these.

Sustained individual 'success', whatever our motives, is quite simply a figment of the imagination. If I don't expect to fail some of the time, I'm just not being realistic. And, more to the point for the people I lead, if I paint an image of Christian living – and Christian leadership – that makes no allowance for human frailty, but demands constant superhuman success, then I'm not only setting them up for extreme disappointment, but virtually ensuring that I run them into the ground.

It's not that sin doesn't matter – in fact, it's precisely because it *does* matter that it's such a mistake for us to keep our weaknesses and our areas of temptation hidden, pretending to other people (and often even to ourselves) that they're not really there. Self-denial of this kind just sets us up for a fall. I need to ensure that I'm a lot more transparent; open and honest with people about my struggles as well as my successes; my weaknesses as well as my strengths.

'Success', once said Winston Churchill, 'is the ability to go from one failure to another with no loss of enthusiasm.' I agree. And the reason I can do it with confidence – indeed, the only reason I've survived as a Christian, let alone a Christian leader, is because of God's grace. I know it's a scandal, but it's my only hope.

great leadership is measured by what's left after you're gone

How easy it is to move from fulfilling the role of the enterprising pioneer to that of a stubbornly wedged cork in the bottle!

Life is constantly changing, not just here at Church.co.uk but within Oasis as a whole. Twenty-one years ago Oasis was just a desk, a chair, a phone, a pre-historic second-hand electric type-writer and me. It was sometimes lonely, but it also had its upsides. For instance, it meant that my ideas and opinions were always accepted. They had no rivals. If I didn't dream it and drive it, it just didn't happen. And this meant that I was given all the credit for whatever we achieved. After all, I was the visionary, the founder, the initiator, the strategist, the manager, the administrator, the publicist and the field worker.

> Though I like to think of myself as a pioneer, deep down inside me there lurks a secret settler.

It's very different now, both within Oasis and, more recently, Church.co.uk. We've grown with the arrival of lots of new people, lots of new activities and lots of new projects. But that means new ideas, new methods, new routines, new thinking, new leaders and new staff. And in it all I've faced some demanding personal challenges and had to learn some uncomfortable lessons about myself, like the disturbing realisation that, though I like to think of myself as a pioneer, deep down inside me there lurks a secret settler.

I'm reminded of what John Maxwell called 'The Law of the Lid'. He said that every leader creates 'a glass ceiling', not just for themselves, but for their entire organisation. The height of this lid is determined by their capacity to keep developing. When their ceiling is reached, not only do they get stuck – simply because they decide that they can't progress any further – their organisation gets stuck with them. In this way the attitude of any leader becomes the limiter on their organisation's growth as well as their own development. If they are smart the lid is high, but conversely, if their ceiling is low, everyone suffers. So my leadership ability – for better or worse – determines not only my effectiveness, but also the future development of Oasis as a whole and Church.co.uk in particular. A decidedly worrying thought!

My problem is that I'm plagued by two reoccurring nightmares that represent two equal and opposite fears. The first is this – that ten years from now people will say, 'The problem with that Steve Chalke was that he just didn't know when to let go, take his hands off the steering wheel and let others get on with the job. In the early days Oasis [or Church.co.uk] grew because of his vision, but in the end he almost killed it because he simply couldn't step back – he had to have a finger in every pie.'

I remember that Theodore Roosevelt once said, 'The best executive is the one who has sense enough to pick good people to do what they want done, and self-restraint enough to keep from meddling with them while they do it.' It's a great thought, but one that is easier to agree with than to act on.

My second nightmare is the exact opposite. In this terrifying apparition it's ten years on again, but this time people say, 'The problem with that Steve Chalke was that though he did a good job to start with, he must have got bored because he took his hand off the tiller far too soon. In the early days Oasis [or Church.co.uk] grew because of his vision, but in the end he almost killed it because he simply lost interest – he just didn't seem to have the staying power that would have allowed the organisation [church] to realise its potential.'

I remember seeing one of those David Attenborough–style natural history programmes on the TV about a herd of some kind of wild horse where the dominant female had been killed in a lion attack. The commentator explained that this death was a tragedy for the whole herd because, robbed of its natural leader before time, the other females would jostle for position and, leaderless, the entire group would struggle to survive the dangers of the long hard winter ahead.

Here is my dilemma – I feel that I'm caught betwixt and between. What do I hand on? What do I keep? Who do I hand it on to? When and how do I do it?

I'm often troubled by the image of that herd of horses. Was it a lesson from heaven warning me not to let go too soon, or a message from hell playing to my inflated sense of self-importance? I'm confused because all this is complicated by another problem. I have to confess that I don't think that I've ever done anything from a pure motive. So, alongside my higher reasons for wrestling with all this 'succession' stuff, I have to be honest enough to admit that I sometimes find myself haunted by the fear of losing significance and stepping into obscurity.

> I need to learn the grace to watch those I work with make mistakes whilst biting my tongue.

It's easy to convince myself that others can't do the job as well as I can; that I've got the maturity and insight that comes with experience that others lack. To complicate it all, some of that is obviously true. I have got more experience than the team

I work with – I'm older, I've been around longer, I've had longer to learn from my mistakes. But again, life is about a lot more than the perfect performances of polished professionals. That's the hallmark of a careless corporation not a caring community. I need to learn the grace to watch those I work with make mistakes whilst biting my tongue, smiling and, at the right moment, offering honest feedback, encouragement and help without falling into one of those patronising 'I told you so' attitudes.

How will history remember me? The jury is out. What kind of lid do I have? How high or low is my ceiling? They say that great leadership is measured by what's left after you're gone. So as I walk what sometimes feels like a tight rope, please Lord, help me to keep my balance.

individualism is the enemy of individuality

Here is a truth that my critics see clearly but has taken me half a lifetime to acknowledge – I am not balanced. I never have been balanced. I never will be balanced. I am incapable of balance. It is painful to admit to myself, let alone anyone else. It is even more painful to commit it to paper. In fact, it feels like the very process of writing it down, recording it so starkly in black and white, makes it truer. And the act of reading back what I've just scribbled somehow seals it as being set in stone.

I am not taking the lazy option, an 'it's just the way I am … you can't teach an old dog new tricks' approach to life. It is just that, try as I might (and I have tried very hard for a very long time) I am, in the end, me. Nothing more, nothing less.

My whole personality – the way in which God has wired me – means that I see things in a particular way, from a specific angle, through a unique set of lenses, which, though they help bring some things into sharp focus, also create some serious blind spots.

> The sobering truth is that my strengths are, at one and the same time, also my weaknesses.

The sobering truth is that my strengths are, at one and the same time, also my weaknesses. An honest self-assessment tells me that my strong points are, in other contexts, my short-comings. My pluses are also my minuses – the very traits that serve me so well in some situations combine to become my 'Achilles heel' in others. I am fifty years old and I'm limping.

But while recognising my lack of balance can feel limiting, it is also a great liberation. When understood correctly an awareness of my limitations, far from crushing me, feels like a thousand ton weight has fallen from my shoulders. I am released from the endless struggle to be what, blatantly, I am not and can never be. I feel free to be me. My goal in life is no longer to attain balance; to be the all-rounder that over the years so many have urged, exhorted and pressurised me to become. Any balance I achieve is found, and will continue to be found, only as part of a community. I am finally learning that individualism is always the enemy of individuality. It is in community that I can be most me.

I have a friend who worked for years as an executive in an extremely well known leadership training company. A few years ago they carried out some research with a group of call-centre workers who all completed a specially developed training course designed to build and improve their skills. Both before and after the course, however, their individual performances were assessed and graded. The findings were revealing. The top 10 percent of workers improved their performance by an average of over 50 percent, the middle 80 percent by an average of around 10 percent, while the bottom 10 percent showed absolutely no improvement at all.

Years ago I heard a well-known church leader explain, 'You can't put into a person what isn't there.' I remember feeling shocked. How could he be so harsh and dismissive? But over the years I have come to see that he was right. The hardest thing in life is to come to terms with who we are.

'You can't put into a person what isn't there' – a church leader

Many people never do. In order to thrive I know that I must accept who I am and who I am not.

Almost twenty-five years ago I was ordained as a Baptist minister. I still remember the promises I made to the duly assembled congregation as I pledged 'to execute [my] charge with all fidelity, to preach and teach the word of God from the Holy Scriptures, to lead the congregation in worship and administer the gospel sacraments, to tend the flock of Christ and to do the work of an evangelist', as well as 'to be faithful in prayer and in the reading and study of the Holy Scriptures, and to lead a life worthy of the calling to which [I had] been called.'

Even as the list of duties was read aloud, I remember wondering

> 'Always listen to your worst enemies as well as your best friends. They are both telling you the truth, but from slightly different perspectives' – Winston Churchill

why nobody was laughing. It felt a bit like that part in the wedding service where the vicar asks the congregation, 'Does anyone know of any lawful impediment why this man may not be joined in holy matrimony to this woman?' I was sure that my mum or one of my mates was just about to jump up and shout, 'Stop, stop, you are all making a huge mistake. Him – a wise counsellor, a sensitive pastor, a tenacious prayer, an informed teacher, and all those other things? You've got the wrong bloke!'

'Always listen to your worst enemies as well as your best friends. They are both telling you the truth, but from slightly different perspectives', said Winston Churchill. Good advice. My critics are right – I do suffer from the shortcomings they so regularly accuse me of. My response, however, is simply this: 'I may walk with a limp, but I'm leaning on my friends.'

approach every problem with an open mind rather than an open mouth

A few years ago I did a stint presenting a live chat show for a commercial radio station. Each evening we would take phone calls from listeners across the UK who would ring in with their often extraordinarily outspoken views on the big news stories of the day. To avoid being sued, the station operated a seven-second delay system that allowed us, when absolutely necessary, to edit out offensive and libellous comments.

If only I had a personal, inbuilt seven-second delay system with which I could achieve the same effect. How many times would such a device have saved those around me from the damaging impact of the things that I unthinkingly rattle off. At my best my words can be like balm – bringing comfort and healing. But just as often, they are like weapons – wounding and bruising. I am constantly amazed that I'm capable of rising so high and sinking so low, all in the same day.

I'm fascinated by those TV chat-show interviews in which a celebrity answers the question 'Do you have any regrets?' with the mind blowing statement that if they could 'do it all again' they 'wouldn't change a thing'. Can they possibly be serious? If I could change the way that I've done

If only I had a personal, inbuilt seven-second delay system.

today I would. If I could turn back time by a couple of hours, I would. If I could suck my words back into my mouth, I would. But it's a bit like the 'Recall This Message' option on a computer for getting back those emails that you've sent by mistake and then wished you hadn't – it's impossible!

I was once extolling the benefits of my idea for a personal seven-second delay system to a friend over a glass of wine. She had two observations. First, she agreed that I would be greatly helped by such technology – which, I have to confess, I was worried she did slightly too readily! Second, she insisted, a little more reassuringly, that I wasn't alone. For all my failings I was in some pretty famous company. For instance, she claimed, Moses might have even made the Promised Land if he'd had a few seconds to make good his error of hitting the rock. A slight delay might have also turned things around for Samson. The same goes for Simon Peter who suffered from more than one very bad outbreak of 'open mouth before engaging brain' syndrome. Paul may have benefited from a little time to reflect before being quite so harsh on Barnabas and John Mark. And things could have been completely turned around for Ananias and Sapphira – if anyone ever needed a seven-second delay system it was them!

I had to admit these were very good points, though the reality is that, as ideal as it would be, neither I nor anyone else can have a fail-safe automatic delay mechanism. That means I need to learn a new discipline instead – the self-imposed delay! There are some things that are best left unsaid, some responses that are best left unmade, some letters that are best left unsent and some information that is best left unshared.

I'm told that Harold Wilson once quipped, 'Politicians are people who approach every question with an open mouth and a closed mind.' My goal, so often unfulfilled, is exactly the reverse – to approach every problem with an open mind rather than an open mouth.

I remember being told the story of Lord Coggan, the former Archbishop of Canterbury, who when asked why he would sit for such long periods in business meetings without commenting replied, 'I try to speak only when I believe that my words will add something to the silence rather than subtract something from it.'

I was recently reading through one of those weekend supplements when my eyes bumped into that famous and oft quoted verse from Ecclesiastes, 'For everything there is a season ... A time to keep silence, and a time to speak.' A good principle but the problem is knowing which applies when. I needed more help. Then, to my surprise, a few pages later, I stumbled across some more wise advice, this time from a less likely source. In the words of British comedian Bob Monkhouse, 'Silence is golden – it's seldom misquoted.' So from now on, I'm aiming to deliver a little more open mind and a little less open mouth.

> 'Silence is golden – it's seldom misquoted'
> – Bob Monkhouse

admiration works best from a distance

We all save our worst behaviour for indoors. It's painful to acknowledge, but that doesn't make it any less true. There's often a gap, a very large gap, between the 'public me' and the 'private me'. I may look like the 'real thing' on the outside – solid oak – but behind my extremely thin veneer there's an awful lot of chipboard lurking.

I spoke at a conference for Christian social activists. After my talk, a man with a very earnest, almost constipated, expression on his face, strode up to me and pressed a sealed envelope into my hand. Having explained what an honour it was to meet me, he informed me that it contained a 'word' that God had charged him to deliver to me personally. I thanked him and pushed it into my back pocket of my trousers and forgot about it.

> There's often a gap, a very large gap, between the 'public me' and the 'private me'.

Yesterday evening I was sitting in our lounge with my wife, Cornelia, and a large cup of coffee and a snack which she had prepared for me. The TV was on. Wearing that same pair of trousers, it was then that I suddenly remembered the envelope. I felt for it, dug it out, tore it open, sat back again and proceeded to read it to myself. 'Mighty man of God,' my prophetic note proclaimed, 'You are the Lord's instrument for this moment. You shall be called a spokesman for his people; an ambassador to kings and queens; a prophet to the nations, for you are one who understands the times.' It concluded with Esther 1:13, 'It was customary for the king to consult experts in matters of law and justice, he spoke with the wise men who understood the times.'

For someone who is supposed to 'understand the times', what happened over the next few minutes was, to say the least, disappointing. According to Cornelia, I made the unfortunate mistake of leaving my prophetic letter, and the screwed up envelope it came in, on the coffee table along with the empty coffee mug, the plate I'd just eaten a cheese sandwich off and the skin of a satsuma. This, she claimed, was after I had spent the previous half an hour ignoring her, staring mindlessly at the TV and intermittently re-reading the prophetic (or did I hear her say 'pathetic'?) letter.

Having made her big point, I noticed that she still picked it up and read it for herself – which if I'm honest, was probably exactly what I was hoping for. Her reaction, however, was definitely not. At first she laughed – she said that it was obviously some kind of a mistake and that perhaps the writer had me confused with Billy Graham. Slightly hurt, I retorted that I couldn't see what was so funny and that I wasn't anything like Billy Graham. 'That's exactly your problem', she quipped, adding, 'whoever wrote that thing should try living with you for a while. Perhaps clearing up the mess you leave behind might sober their judgement a bit. Ambassador to the nations – you don't often make it as far as the kitchen sink!'

I didn't think it was wise to point out to Cornelia that the note actually said that I'd be an ambassador to kings and queens, not just to the nations! So much for the impact of the prophetic word – like they say, admiration always works best from a distance. Still, I'm encouraged by the story that I've often heard told of Ruth Graham, the wife of the famous American evangelist Billy Graham. When asked about whether she had ever considered divorcing her busy husband, she answered, 'Divorce never – murder often!'

'Choosing Consistency, Resisting Compromise' is the strap line of *Who You Are When No One's Looking*, the best-selling book by Bill Hybels. It's a great goal but somehow the gap between the person I long to be and the one that I am – the gap between my aspiration and my achievement – never seems to narrow, especially at home.

A few years ago, when our children were all still at school, I got myself into the habit of getting up early each morning and taking the short walk up to our local park to sit on a bench by the pond, read the Bible and pray in the stillness. I did this consistently for a couple of months at the beginning of one summer and was really pleased with myself. It was such an uplifting way to start each day – soaking in God's presence and peace. But, how well I remember the day when, on arriving home for a spot of breakfast before heading off to the office, Cornelia, rather than celebrating my newly developed spiritual appetite, suddenly exploded. Every morning I had been sitting there, smugly nurturing my devotional life and reflecting on the finer points of the challenge of world mission, while she was left to wash, dress, feed and get our four kids ready for school, single-handedly. For her, there was little opportunity to start the day reflecting on anything other than why her bone-idle husband had chosen to abandon her yet again.

> 'He who is too busy doing good finds no time to be good'
> – Rabindranath Tagore

'He who is too busy doing good finds no time to be good', once remarked Rabindranath Tagore, a winner of the Nobel Prize for Literature. Perhaps that was his way of confessing to the fact that, like me, he tended to save his worst behaviour for indoors.

trust evolves – it is never a simple 'on' or 'off' affair

Eighteen months or so after I started work at Church.co.uk, Waterloo, Margaret, who is in her mid-eighties, cornered me after a morning service and complained, 'I'm not happy ... I'm not very happy at all.'

I remember that, at one and the same time, I was hurt but also felt that I couldn't really blame her. Margaret, I knew, had been part of Church.co.uk, Waterloo since long before it was called Church.co.uk, Waterloo – probably since before I was born. I also knew that she was a widow and that her beloved husband, Paul, had served for many years as a church leader here until his death. I'd watched Margaret as she sat in services that touched on themes like marriage or grief and listened to her as she chatted when she came into our coffee shop during the week. I knew that she was aching because she missed Paul so much and longed, with all her heart for the joy of days gone by. There's a haunting line in the song 'Empty Chairs' from the musical *Les Misérables*: 'Oh my friends, my friends forgive me, that I live and you are gone. There's a grief that can't be spoken. There's a pain goes on and on.' Those lyrics seem to sum up Margaret's situation pretty well.

'Trust no one unless you have eaten much salt with him' – Cicero

Being part of Church.co.uk is a bittersweet experience for Margaret. Even its new fangled name must be almost incomprehensible to someone who has never used a computer, let alone the Internet, in her life. For Margaret, I know that our church – her church – acts as an important point of contact with her past. And I know that, in some ways, the changes that I felt I had to introduce, when I arrived two and a half years ago, had the effect of cutting her umbilical cord with those precious memories.

Recently a church leader sat in my office and complained bitterly about how his 'ministry' had been 'smashed' by his congregation's 'blind and unthinking loyalty to dead and irrelevant tradition'. As a result, he claimed that he had found himself isolated and rejected. I tried to suggest, that he might have misjudged the reason for his situation. In my experience, it's far more often a lack of respect for, and love of, people on which 'ministries' are wrecked. It's only as people get to know you that they are able to place their trust in you and journey with you to unfamiliar and strange places. As Cicero put it way back in the first century BC: 'Trust no one unless you have eaten much salt with him.'

'To be trusted is a greater compliment than to be loved' – George MacDonald

I have learnt that building trust is a time-consuming business. It requires a lot of hard and sustained work. Trust evolves; it is never a simple 'on' or 'off' affair. It can't be rushed and it can't be hurried. It has to be earned. It develops slowly, growing, rather than just appearing. There is simply no shortcut to securing it. In the words of George MacDonald, the Victorian novelist, poet and church leader, 'To be trusted is a greater compliment than to be loved.' As hard as it is to achieve, however, this prized commodity is vital to every church leader especially in a time of cultural transition.

I often think that trust is like money in the bank: though one withdrawal will not necessarily take me into the red, if over time funds only flow out, eventually even the richest account will be emptied. The reverse is also true: the more deposits I make, however small, the more credit I collect. In other words, the building or breakdown of trust is normally incremental. Although in extreme cases an act of betrayal is enough to destroy it immediately, most of the time its ebb and flow are gradual.

> She looked me in the eye and gently said, 'I'm happy … I'm very happy indeed. I trust you.'

But the lesson it has taken me decades to get into my thick head is that trust is emotional every bit as much as it is rational. It is never simply a matter of cold intellectual understanding; it is just as much an emotional response to someone as it is to their ideas.

I know that Margaret still doesn't like a lot of the songs we use – I don't expect that she ever will; I know that the informality of the way I dress would still not be her first choice – for her it lacks a certain sense of reverence and respect; I know that the newly installed drum-kit will never fill the gap left by our abandonment of the organ. Indeed, I am sure that there are a 101 little things that Margaret would choose to be different about our services.

But recently Margaret cornered me again and proceeded to ask an extraordinarily blunt question, 'Are you planning to leave?' she demanded to know. My heart sank. But I drew a deep breath and decided to tell her the truth anyway. 'No', I announced as emphatically as I could. Then it happened. Margaret smiled an honest and unguarded smile. She looked me in the eye and gently said, 'I'm happy … I'm very happy indeed. I trust you.' I smiled back, a relieved and grateful smile. I held her hand and said, 'Thank you.'

praise is the miracle tool

'People are not changed by moral exhortation but by transformed imagination', wrote Walter Brueggemann. I couldn't agree more. So why, I ask myself, am I still, after all these years, so sluggish when it comes to doing anything about it? Why aren't I more generous with my thanks? Why am I slow to express enthusiastic appreciation? Why do I so often miss the moment to show gratitude? Why do I tend to minimise the positives and maximise the negatives? Why do I damn with faint praise when I could build up with wholehearted affirmation?

The other day, someone – a friend who is a passionate, committed and an extremely hard working servant of Church. co.uk – told me about an idea they had and an arrangement they had made as a result. My heart sank. In an instant I could see all the problems that their plan could potentially create. I felt the blood rush to my head (a sure sign that I am losing perspective and in danger of saying something I will regret) but didn't stop to heed my instinct. Instead I heard a number of very badly chosen sentences, all too readily betraying my sense of panic and disapproval, leave my mouth. I then had to attempt to paste over them with some hastily

Why aren't I more generous with my thanks?

manufactured faint praise of the sort that can freeze the heart as readily as outright blame.

The ridiculous thing is that a few years ago I wrote a chapter in a book about the stupidity of what I called 'the management technique of nagging and yelling'. In it I said that when you shout or nag at people to get things done, all you actually do is eat away gradually at their enthusiasm to do anything. Eventually they'll come to resent your comments (and, of course, you!), so much that you'll get nothing more than the bare minimum out of them. 'Tearing people off a strip' is the worst possible way of getting them to learn from their mistakes. It demotivates rather than motivates. As a tool for inspiring change, it's about as effective as trying to start a fire with a bucket of ice cold water. On the other hand, if you learn to praise people for the good work they do or the effort they make, they start to feel good about themselves and want to achieve more. And as their confidence grows, they'll do an even better job – creating a virtuous cycle rather than a vicious circle. I concluded that even when you've got to confront a short-sighted decision or poor performance, it's far more effective to do so within the context of praise for what has been done well, or at the very least, the commitment that has been made. To say that the expression 'Those who can, do, and those who can't, teach', has been at the forefront of my mind over the last few days is something of an understatement.

'The days that make us happy, make us wise', I happened to read, bleary eyed, in the newspaper this morning. We all do our best when we feel good about ourselves and we feel good about ourselves when we're told we're doing well. Praise helps people recognise and build on what they can do, and to work harder to overcome their weaknesses. That's why praise is the miracle tool.

Mao Tse Tung, the former Chinese leader, once claimed, 'Power grows out of the barrel of a gun.' As far as he was concerned, fear was the most reliable way of ensuring that you got what you wanted from people. They would do whatever you told them to if they were sufficiently afraid of the consequences of not doing it. However, I remember that Martin Luther King, another world leader, had a very different approach. He called love 'the most durable power in the world'. The problem for me isn't that I can't make up my mind about who and what to believe. It's just that being committed to the principle is not the same thing as being consistent about the practice.

Just as a flower blossoms when you give it enough water and dies when you neglect it, so a person's self-confidence will bloom when you praise them and wither when you don't. Experts call this the Law of Reinforcement – 'behaviour which achieves desirable consequences will recur.' We all like to feel valued and appreciated. So if you praise me when I do something right, I'll be more likely to do it again. And if you praise me for putting in the effort, I'll want to try just as hard, if not harder, in the future.

> A person's self-confidence will bloom when you praise them.

A wise man by the name of John Wooden once said, 'You can't let praise or criticism get to you. It's a weakness to get caught up in either one.' He's right of course, but I've yet to meet the person who is self-confident and mature enough to pull it off.

So, when I saw my friend again earlier today, I managed to summon the courage to apologise for my behaviour the other day and my half-hearted response to his idea. I told him that his hard work, energy and ongoing commitment were examples not only to me but to so many others at Church.co.uk. He thanked me and then proceeded to ask what advice I could give him about his suggestion and what I thought would be the wisest way ahead, as he was keen to learn from me and get on with the job. If only I'd have done it that way the first time round. The experts are right – praise is the miracle tool.

keep the main thing, the main thing

'The world is changed. I feel it in the water. I feel it in the earth. I smell it in the air', announced Galadriel the elf in the prologue to the movie adaptation of Tolkien's *The Fellowship of the Ring*. Here at Church.co.uk it's also time for change. It's daunting, but I can feel it.

A few years ago I had the opportunity to spend a day with Dr. Billy Graham in New York. We spent most of it in a hotel room talking. Towards the end of our time together I asked him if there was one piece of wisdom, beyond all others, that he would like to pass on to me. We were sat opposite each other in big armchairs. He thought for a moment, then leant forward and whispered, 'Life goes quickly.' My facial expression must have given away that I was expecting something more, because he looked at me and simply repeated the same three words: 'Life goes quickly', before adding, 'much more quickly than you are expecting.'

> 'Life goes quickly … much more quickly than you are expecting' – Billy Graham

'The main thing is to keep the main thing, the main thing', the saying goes. And because I believe what Billy Graham said, I want to live the years I have left – however many or few that might be – 'on purpose'.

It was a summer afternoon, 28 August 1963, and a crowd of about a quarter of a million people had gathered in Washington, D.C. Martin Luther King Jr. stood on the steps of the Lincoln Memorial. On that day he would make what would become the greatest speech of his life; a speech, the text of which is now available on countless postcards and in endless books; which according to Google, is referred to 7,810,000 times on the internet; a speech which, without doubt, is the most remembered of the twentieth century.

'I have a dream', King cried. Yet I am convinced that at this, his greatest moment, he was selling himself short. I've been around long enough to know that everyone dreams. Indeed, we live in a world packed full of dreamers. But dreams are cheap – they cost nothing – and are soon gone. All too often they evaporate in the searing heat of reality just as surely as the dew evaporates in the burning sun.

Over the years I have met countless dreamers. Young and old, male and female, rich and poor – they come in all sorts of shapes and sizes, ages and guises. But Martin Luther King wasn't one of them – he was a visionary.

> A dreamer's ideas float, then dissolve and disappear; a visionary's ideas stick around.

A dreamer's ideas float, then dissolve and disappear; a visionary's ideas stick around. A visionary's ideas get out of their owner's head and into their arms, into their hands, their fingers, legs, feet and toes. A visionary's ideas move them, drive them, motivate them and inspire them. A visionary's ideas wake them up early in the morning, keep them up late at night and leave them wrestling, worrying, working and praying until they are fulfilled. Whereas a dream flatters the dreamer, a vision hurts. Vision demands laser-like focus, dogged determination and unwavering dedication. Or, to put it differently, vision is about working to 'keep the main thing the main thing'.

So what is my vision? What am I dedicated to achieving? I am passionate about working to bring transformation – spiritually, socially, emotionally, physically and environmentally – to marginalised people. I want to see both individuals and whole communities liberated by hope. I want to help people discover a life-changing relationship with Christ. In the years I have left, I want to achieve maximum impact, maximum influence and leave behind holistic churches that are strong, effective and robust.

I am, along with the whole team here at Oasis, committed to planting and sustaining a network of Church.co.uk churches in urban priority areas. The problem is, however, that we can't do that and still keep things the way that they are here. I'm scared; we're all scared; but growth means challenge and change – and both are uncomfortable.

So after two-and-a-half-years of working to develop Church. co.uk, Waterloo, I am stepping down as its senior minister and will hand over to my friend Dave, who is currently on our staff. I am then going to be commissioned as the Church.co.uk network leader.

This change of roles means that Dave will be taking on the responsibility for leading the future development of the congregation here in Waterloo. I will give my time to mentoring him as he takes the reins, as well as to launching and developing other Church.co.uk churches. It is a huge challenge. It will be a big stretch for me and for us all, but faith is a dynamic journey, not a dead doctrine, and we don't want to get complacent. We are intimidated, but we are determined not to get distracted.

My prayer is this: 'Lord, grant me the vision to see; the faith to believe; the courage to do.' Or, 'Life goes quickly, so help us to keep the main thing, the main thing.'

people follow people not disembodied principles

'Never oversell yourself', my mother warned me. Well, I was recently introduced as 'Steve Chalke, the leader of the Church. co.uk Network'. Though technically accurate, this extremely impressive title is rather misleading, by virtue of the fact that it glosses over one very significant detail: the network I lead consists of just one church. I am, without doubt, the leader of the smallest network of churches in the universe!

Making the decision to work towards the development of a network of, what we plan to be 360 degree churches – Christ centred communities whose mission is to bring whole life regeneration and well-being to individuals as well as entire neighbourhoods – is one thing, achieving it is something else altogether.

I know that at one level my responsibility is simply to take the first step of faith. Neither I nor any one else in Oasis is able to see the whole staircase before we start climbing. But, that said, (changing the metaphor just slightly) if you begin a walk of 1,000 miles by heading just a couple of degrees away from your true course, by the time you've gone the whole distance, you are bound to end up many miles from your real destination. Mistakes are magnified by scale.

Mistakes are magnified by scale.

89

change agents

In fact, I asked a mathematically minded friend of mine to work out just how many miles I would be off target on a 1,000 mile march if I began it by facing a couple of degrees in the wrong direction. Having punched all sorts of numbers into the calculator on his phone, he announced emphatically, '34.92.' So if my life to this point has been an intensive training course for the road ahead, what has it taught me that will help me accurately chart this next leg of the journey – the planting of new churches in marginalised communities?

One of the most important things I've learnt over the years is that in church life – just as in every other area – it is, in the end, the quality of leadership that is the key to all else. People follow people not disembodied principles. The people of Israel followed Moses out of slavery, not just the concept of freedom. Generations later it was Nehemiah who inspired them to rebuild the walls of Jerusalem, not just the idea of national honour.

> The people of Israel followed Moses out of slavery, not just the concept of freedom.

Sometime ago a friend of mine told me about a prophecy that he had just heard from a member of his local church. 'The Lord has finished with using personalities' – instead he has 'chosen to do a new thing'. He asked me what my reaction to this shock announcement from the Almighty was. I made the point that if God was planning such a course of action, it would represent a major break with his chosen method of operation, not only for the entire biblical period, but also the subsequent history of the church to date. From Gideon to Gumble, Nathan to Nightingale, Peter to Pullinger, Timothy to Tyndale and Paul to Pilavachi, God has always used personalities to lead and I believe he always will.

At the heart of building the Church.co.uk Network is the task of finding and training strong leaders. But even the best leaders can't function where they are not granted genuine authority or space to get on with the job. I grew up in Baptist churches amid stories of ministers who were bullied and manipulated by obstinate organists, demented deacons and militant members. It's a good thing that when God created the rainbow he didn't have to consult a church members meeting or he might still be struggling to get the colours finalised. Though a wise leader will always listen to and reflect on the views and opinions of a wide variety of people, a strong church is not a democracy. With the responsibility of leadership, there must be granted the authority to lead.

However, I've also learned that, in the end, churches suffer if and when their leaders are allowed to become unaccountable. If the biggest problem in some churches is that you feel like standing up to shout, 'Will someone, anyone, please lead us somewhere?' – in others the problem is exactly the opposite. 'I'm accountable to God!' is nothing more than a spiritual sound-ing spin on, 'I do what I like, so don't you dare challenge me'.

Way back in 1631, John Donne, the then Dean of St. Paul's Cathedral, wrote, 'No man is an island, entire of itself; every man is a piece of the continent, a part of the main.' But the best part of 400 years later, all too often, his words are unheeded. If alongside the responsibility of leadership must sit the author-ity and freedom to lead, with that authority there must also exist a system which ensures well-defined and genuine lines of accountability.

So how will I hold our leaders to account, challenge them and ask them the hard questions, but at the same time encourage, coach and affirm them? How will I mentor them in their personal development, monitor their performance and yet leave room for them to be themselves? And, lastly, the biggest question of them all – if it is true that people follow people and not disem-bodied principles and I am the leader of this fledgling network, how will I ensure that I continue to be held accountable too?

inclusion never demands conformity

An encounter of a depressing kind – that's what I'd call the conversation I found myself in after yesterday morning's service. If I'm honest, I could see it coming from the moment he walked through the door. Everything about this rather severe looking, middle-aged man – from the earnest expression on his face to his appalling choice of knitwear – instantly telegraphed his intentions. No sooner had the words of the closing prayer left my lips than my worst suspicions were confirmed. Our wool-clad visitor, who had until then been sitting at the back of the building clutching a large Bible and notebook in which he scribbled furiously throughout my sermon, strode towards me armed with an expression of righteous indignation. It was a frightening sight – a little like an assault from some kind of latter-day conquistador.

'The Lord has sent me to you with a message of judgement …'

As we talked, or to put it more accurately, as I listened, he made it clear that he'd paid us this 'special visit' in order to 'weigh' our theology. 'The Lord has sent me to you with a message of judgement', he trumpeted. 'He calls you to repent and turn back to him.' Obviously the 'weighing' process was already complete and had not gone well!

The heart of our rebellion, he said, had been exposed as I had outlined the five core values around which we are aiming to build the network of new Church.co.uk churches. As part of my sermon I had explained, what we think of as the five *I*'s of an 'intelligent church' – Intimacy, Involvement, Influence, Inter-dependence and Inclusion. Perhaps, as I had already guessed, it was the last one – the one about inclusion – that had really upset him. 'We will serve and respect all people regardless of their gender, marital status, race, ethnic origin, religion, age, sexual orientation or physical and mental capability', I had said.

'What you are doing is a disgrace – the Church is called to uphold godly standards', he barked in conclusion. Then, turning his back on me, he exited with as great a sense of purpose as he had arrived in the first place. I swear I could see him attempting to shake the dust off his feet as he went – or perhaps it was just the awkward way that his ill fitting open-toed sandals forced him to walk.

Why is it that I only ever come up with those smart, one-line responses when it's too late? I've replayed the few minutes I spent in the presence of my self-appointed judge a hundred times in the last twenty-four hours and have crafted a variety of cutting retorts that if I'd delivered at the time, would have buried him. On reflection, it's probably a good thing that I'm slower off the mark than I'd like to be.

Inclusion never demands conformity. Agreement is not a condition of acceptance. It seems to me that for Jesus this was a foundational principle of his whole approach to life. Perhaps the ultimate example of which is his relationship with Judas. Judas shared some of Jesus' most intimate moments; he was one of the inner community of twelve. For anyone looking in from the outside his relationship with Jesus would have appeared, superficially at least, extremely close. But scratch beneath the surface and you'd soon discover that he was heading away from Jesus rather than being drawn closer. Though he was travelling in the wrong direction, however, the Gospels don't make even the slightest suggestion that he was distrusted or held at arm's length. In fact he was included by Jesus just as much as the other disciples. That he would ultimately betray his mentor for a handful of coins doesn't seem to have limited his relationship with Jesus before the event. Though eventually Judas opted out of relationship with Jesus, he was the one who had to make that decision. But more than that, it seems that Jesus deliberately left the door open for Judas as long as possible. Extraordinarily he even chose to wash his betrayer's feet and to share a meal with him at the very last moment, rather than reject him.

Paradoxically, yesterday's visitor was right. The Church must 'uphold godly standards'. The deeper question, however, is this: Which standards are God's standards? A few years ago, I heard a well known preacher claim, 'Our biggest mistake is that we have been dogmatic about that which we should have been agnostic, and agnostic about that which we should have been dogmatic.'

> It seems that Jesus deliberately left the door open for Judas as long as possible.

I'm convinced that the standard we are called to uphold beyond all others is that of grace. Is what we are doing a disgrace? I believe that it is a lack of inclusiveness which is literally a 'dis-grace'. The Church is called to model the phenomenon of undeserved acceptance. Put simply, our task is to be the indisputable proof that God is love.

We want to build churches that are inclusive and welcoming to all. Churches where you are in until you jump out, rather than out until you jump in. That means that Church.co.uk churches will be messy – Waterloo already is. Why? Because messiness is a consequence of inclusion. Indeed, whenever a local church chooses to be outward looking and welcoming of all, it will automatically become messier than it was before – it's inevitable. If we take Jesus as our model and invest ourselves in the lives of others as he did, our churches will never be neat, tidy or orderly again. The very act of inclusion necessarily dictates that our churches will be comprised of a diverse collection of people at different points on the journey of faith. They will not believe the same things. They will not have the same values. They will not behave consistently.

'If it's neat, quiet and orderly that you're after, the graveyard is your only option.'

I once heard an old man comment, 'If it's neat, quiet and orderly that you're after, the graveyard is your only option.' I think he was probably right.

nothing is so simple that it cannot be misunderstood

'There must be a less miserable way of being poor than this', I heard a church leader sigh recently. His words resonated with me. I felt his pain. I understood. I empathised. And his sad but comic phrase has echoed around my head ever since. So although perhaps I shouldn't, I'm going to indulge myself just for a moment or two. I've got some stuff to get off my chest, and I hope that scribbling it down will, in some way, prove cathartic.

Someone that I spend a lot of time working very hard to help complained that they felt undermined by me. Half an hour later, another friend casually remarked that he sees me as a guy with good people skills who is just too busy to use them. That was a clever one; the mother of all backhanded compliments – and the straw that finally broke this camel's back. I'm tired. I'm busy. I'm fed up. I'm overworked. I'm exhausted. I'm exasperated. I feel overwhelmed and undervalued.

> Another friend … sees me as a guy with good people skills who is just too busy to use them.

It seems like nothing I do is so simple that it can't be misunderstood. Am I condemned to spend my life working myself into the ground for people intent on misreading my motives, misinterpreting my actions and, no doubt, misrepresenting my character behind my back?

Reading the last couple of paragraphs back to myself is a shock. I realise that they amount to the equivalent of one of those letters or emails that you might occasionally write but should never send. Scribbling my thoughts down may have been cathartic, but rereading them is horrific. What my writing does tell me very clearly, however, is that I'm in a bad way. In fact, I'm probably becoming slightly paranoid.

Whenever I end up feeling like this I think again about the story of Jesus that John 13 records. For me it's one of the most challenging passages in the entire New Testament. John explains that Jesus did an extraordinary thing – he washed the smelly and sweaty feet of his argumentative, self-seeking and often ungrateful friends. Jesus, God incarnate, knelt on a dusty floor and bathed twelve pairs of filthy feet – including the pair that belonged to the man he knew would betray him within a few hours. Where on earth did he find the strength to do that? John's answer, contained in verse three, is emphatic: 'Jesus knew that the Father had put all things under his power, and that he had come from God and was returning to God.' Jesus' ability to serve his disciples by washing their feet sprang from his inner strength – he knew who he was and where he was going. Jesus' behaviour was simply the outworking of his internal sense of security.

At any point, the more secure I am within myself, the more relaxed and generous I find that I can be. It is when I feel insecure that I tend to come out fighting instead of loving. Lisa Marie Presley, Elvis' daughter, put it this way, 'I'm like a lion – I roar. If someone betrays me, I won't be a victim. I don't sulk, I get angry. I go immediately into retaliation. But it always comes from insecurity or pain.'

Aggressive outbursts and rash words are invariably symptoms of insecurity – the products of a lack of inner strength.

American president, Jimmy Carter, once commented, 'A strong person can afford to be gentle and restrained. It's a weak person that must behave with bluster and boasting.' Or, as life has slowly taught me, nothing is so simple that it cannot be misunderstood. A tired or hurting person will be easily hurt and easily hurt others.

'Don't complain, don't explain' – that was a piece of advice once given to me, by a good friend when I sought his counsel after hearing what I felt were some unkind and unfair comments about myself. 'You will be misunderstood and misrepresented', he added, 'but don't waste your time and emotional energy fighting back – just smile and move on.' Wise counsel – but unfortunately dependent on a level of inner strength and maturity that often seems to elude me.

> A tired or hurting person will be easily hurt and easily hurt others.

Looking back, I confess that I know exactly what my friend (the one that made the remark about my busyness getting in the way of my people skills) meant, and I realise he'd be horrified if he ever read my diary and saw the way that I'd managed to misrepresent and misconstrue his words. What's more, I know that he's right – I am often too busy to stop and use my people skills. But, most poignantly, the only reason I ever jumped to the wrong conclusion about his comment in the first place is that nothing is so simple that it cannot be misunderstood – especially by someone as prone to insecurity as me.

followers expect easy answers, leaders know there are none

I watched a programme on TV that informed me that, according to the Second Law of Thermodynamics, in a closed system nature tends from order to disorder: 'The entropy of an isolated system not at equilibrium will tend to increase over time approaching a maximum value.' I was so impressed I wrote it down. I never was much good at physics, but science aside, the whole 'entropy thing' could be renamed the Second Law of Church dynamics. Entropy simply describes the inevitable and steady deterioration of any system – society, organisation or church – without a constant supply of external input (new ideas and change).

I sat in on a group we put together to look at some of the big challenges and changes we are facing here at Church.co.uk over the next six months. Rather than yielding any clarity, our conversation did the opposite. The only thing that everyone in the room could agree about is that the way things have been is rapidly coming to an end. The longer the group talked, the more complex and complicated the issues and decisions we were facing seemed to become. 'It's all such a muddle', someone blurted out. 'Let's consolidate before we push ahead like this.'

To be honest, as I looked around the room all I could see were hard

The way forward is always difficult.

choices. The way forward is always difficult. It is full of big risks, but, ironically, as we all recognise in our best moments, the greatest risk of all is to risk nothing. I tried to help the discussion by suggesting that though I didn't think it was possible to achieve clarity yet, if we had the courage to move ahead, in the very act of so doing we would slowly get there, probably sometime in the next few months. Someone else agreed, but then, with a smile, added that even then it would only last for a few weeks before we would find ourselves immersed in a new set of challenges and choices. They were right of course. The pain of constant uncertainty is a given; the only question is whether it's the pain of growing or dying.

The future offers us no security, no warranty against our obsolescence or irrelevance. I have a good friend who is an extremely senior executive in the City of London. I remember him telling me that he regularly explains to his staff, 'I can't guarantee you a job this time next year. There are no guarantees for anyone. But what I can promise is this: if we work hard, are flexible and are ready to embrace constant change, together we can do our best to ensure that we have a place in the new world that is forever dawning.' Alvin Toffler summed it up when he said, 'The illiterates of the 21st century will not be those who cannot read and write but those who cannot learn, unlearn and relearn.'

The call to consolidate sounds plausible enough: 'Give us a moment to catch our breath, reflect and regroup.' The problem is that in reality it often turns out to be little more than an attempt to escape the hard questions of a forever-changing world; a disguise, conscious or unconscious, for the desire for comfort and steady state. We all crave certainty; the bravery, guts and nerve it takes to step out into the unknown are huge. Most of us are conservatives at heart. Consolidation – the development of strength and resources appropriate to the task ahead – is vital, but too often becomes an excuse for taking our foot off the accelerator or, to change the metaphor, sticking our heads in the sand and 'doing an ostrich'. Successful consolidation is actually all about maintaining forward momentum – finding the best way of scoping, shaping and securing the new resources necessary for future growth. I've slowly learnt that the actual process of taking risk, of squaring up to the giant you face, is by far the most effective way of unpicking and clarifying the issues involved.

Why is this? Because in a closed system nature tends from order to disorder. Without a constant supply of external input, new ideas and change, entropy inevitably sets in. Consolidation is not an excuse for stagnation.

'The very survival of Christianity in Europe and America depends upon the emergence of men and women able to think new thoughts and devise new strategies at the real frontiers of mission today', writes David Smith in his book *Mission after Christendom*. But he goes on to explain that such people 'are likely to face misunderstanding, criticism and serious opposition. Like ... generations of pioneering, Spirit-led missionaries before them, those who are ready to confront the challenge posed by Western culture must not be surprised if they are accused of unorthodoxy, even heresy, or are verbally attacked by people who interpret their missionary vision as something liable to undermine the moral purity and integrity of the church of Jesus Christ.'

> 'The kind of thinking that will solve the world's problems will be of a different order to the kind of thinking that created those problems in the first place'
> – Albert Einstein

Like the great astrophysicist Albert Einstein said, 'The kind of thinking that will solve the world's problems will be of a different order to the kind of thinking that created those problems in the first place.' Or to put it differently, followers expect easy answers – leaders know there are none.

no progress without process

'I have orders to be awakened at any time in case of national emergency, even if I'm in a Cabinet meeting', once joked President Ronald Regan. I can identify with that one. I'm allergic to small print, spreadsheets and monthly reports. If I spend too much time in too many committees I begin to suffocate. Too many details bore me. I'm a big-picture thinker: I do the blue-sky thing, I have ideas, I paint with broad brushstrokes, I dream dreams, I have visions. I have to get out there, meet people, network and explore new possibilities.

But this personal lopsidedness has its weaknesses. Vision is essential, but never enough. If you want to make real progress, find yourself someone who can process; someone you really trust who does detail – and find them fast. That's the point I made at a meeting about the way forward as we work to develop the Church.co.uk Network of churches.

No progress without process: it's a lesson I first learned during a crisis that almost killed Oasis (of which Church.co.uk is part) back in the mid-eighties. In the early days, life in the small team that grew around me was exciting (if a little exhausting!). We knew where we were going and we grew fast. But a few years in,

Vision is essential, but never enough.

105

with about ten staff, we began to hit some serious problems. Things had changed: my colleagues weren't as motivated as they once were, and relationships were getting a little stretched and strained. We were hobbling not running.

All this came to a head for me while I was speaking at a conference on leadership. Ironically, I'd been invited to talk on how to grow a healthy organisation. Making the most of being surrounded by speakers who actually knew what they were talking about, I took the opportunity of confiding in one of them. 'I am a fraud', I explained. 'Oasis is history. It's been good – but it's over. After a flying start, we've somehow lost our way. It's just not working anymore. We've prayed about it and even fasted over it. But we're finished. I've just not got what it takes to do the job anymore.'

I instantly regretted having confessed. Suddenly this guy looked more like a whistle-blower than a confidant. I felt sure that by the next day the whole conference would know my secret. And as if to fulfil my worst fears, he reached into his bag, pulled out a Bible and began to read it to me. I remember thinking, 'This is it – the private sermon before the public humiliation.' The story he read was from Acts 6. Having finished, he very purposefully paused, looked straight at me and said, 'Do you get it?' It must have been clear from the blank expression on my face that I did not get it at all. So he explained his point and what he said made such an impact on me that I can remember it to this day.

The story in Acts is all about how the Jerusalem church was growing fast but how as it grew some of its members began to complain 'because their widows were being overlooked in the daily distribution of food.' 'So', my new-found mentor asked, 'what did the apostles do? Does the text tell us that they prayed about it? No. Does it mention that they fasted over it? No. Did they beat themselves up about it? Repent over it? Retreat because of it? No. It says that they gathered the church together, chose seven men who were "known to be full of the Spirit and wisdom" and publicly stated their commitment to "turn this responsibility over to them."

'The apostles understood that their problem wasn't spiritual', my friend smiled, 'it was administrative. As leaders they recognised that they needed reliable and wise help to manage it and to take the pressure off them. And the outcome of having the courage to deal with this resource issue is that, as the story concludes, "the word of God spread. The number of disciples in Jerusalem increased rapidly".'

> 'The apostles understood that their problem wasn't spiritual, ... it was administrative.'

It was like the lights came on inside my head. That was my problem: Oasis had grown fast and all the escalating responsibility, not just for our overall direction but for too much of the detail, was resting on me.

The terms *leadership* and *management* are often used interchangeably, but they actually describe two very different sets of responsibilities – which means that good leaders are not necessarily good managers and visa versa. A leader's core function is to set new direction and spearhead the advance. A manager's task is to organise resources (including people), according to principles and values that have already been established, in order to take and hold the new ground. So whereas leadership without management will inevitably cripple an organisation by overstretching and even exploding it, management without leadership is as likely to eventually collapse in on itself, destroying it through implosion.

For me, this revelation was a revolution, which is why, many years later, the first person I appointed to work with me at Church.co.uk wasn't an assistant minister, youth worker, pastoral visitor, evangelist or community worker, but a manager

to get things (including me!) organised. And it's why, following our 'way forward' meeting, I'm happy to say, we took the
wise decision to find a good Church.co.uk Network manager
as quickly as possible.

you can't do what you can't imagine

'The dumbest people in the world', I read in a weekend magazine, 'are those who are sure they know everything. Their self-assured certainty not only pits them against one another but, worse still, it prevents them from learning anything new. They are, by definition, truly ignorant!' Now there's something to think about.

Today we had had another of our now-regular meetings about the development of the Church.co.uk Network – our goal is to begin four new Church.co.uks during the next two years. As part of our preparation for this, over the last couple of months we recruited a team of volunteers to help lead the projects and put a training course together for them. The big questions we now faced all relate to the details of how the relationship between the network and the individual churches will work in the long term. What kind of leadership and governance structures should we develop? How do we build a group of churches with a common ethos as well as shared values and standards? How can we best support our local leaders, holding

> 'No one is stupid enough to pour new wine into old wineskins.' Well, the problem is, perhaps I am!

them accountable yet at the same time giving them the space they need to be themselves?

'If you can't imagine it, you can't do it', observed Albert Einstein. The greatest barrier to the development of any project, including, as I'm discovering, a church network, is its leader's ability to think in new ways and to see things differently.

That's why I live in fear that my imagination, or to be more accurate, lack of it, may end up boxing our fledgling church network into various outmoded, inappropriate and late twentieth century ways of being, shaped more by the baggage of my past experience mixed with my denominational prejudices than a genuine engagement with contemporary culture based on core biblical principles. Jesus once remarked, 'No one is stupid enough to pour new wine into old wineskins.' Well, the problem is, perhaps I am!

Like it or not, any church, charity or initiative I lead will always be limited by the size, scope and flexibility of my imagination. So, as long as I remain the leader of the Church.co.uk Network, I am the cork in its bottle.

As if to rub this disturbing thought in, as I'm sitting here writing, an aging hippy has just strolled past my study window – a cross between Bob Dylan and a latter-day Old Testament prophet – dressed in jeans, open-toed sandals and an extremely garish red T-shirt which, in large letters emblazoned across its front, bore the slogan, 'Everything you know is wrong.'

'The only thing more expensive than education is ignorance' – Benjamin Franklin

I've often thought about Benjamin Franklin's comment, 'The only thing more expensive than education is ignorance.' Why does the man who runs the corner shop I use, and who works every hour under the sun, never succeed in developing his business? Why does the guy who set up in the shop front next door to his, around the same time, now run a chain of stores across London and get more time off? Why does one church always seem to have around the same sized core group, whatever the leaders tell you about how fast it is growing, while another genuinely expands and multiplies?

Michelangelo was not the first sculptor to be given the task of working on a huge block of marble that had been quarried from the Italian Alps. In 1464 Agostino di Duccio had bought the giant rock but, coming to regard it as unstable because of the fault that ran right through it, soon abandoned the project to transform it. Two years later, Antonio Rossellino picked up where Duccio left off. But within months, the problems posed by the massive

> 'What really gets me into trouble is not what I don't know, it's what I know for sure but just isn't so'
> – Mark Twain

block of marble meant that it was, once more, doomed to be discarded – this time for another twenty-five years. It was not until 16 August 1501 that Michelangelo took up the daunting, three-year task of completing what is now the world's most iconic sculpture. 'David', portraying the famous biblical king at the moment he decided to do battle with Goliath, is, without doubt, the most recognisable statue in the history of art.

I want to be a Michelangelo – not a Duccio or Rossellino. What was it that gave Michelangelo the ability to see what others were blind to? And to that end, how do I fuel my imagination? How do I nurture my creativity? How do I feed my mind? How do I keep learning, growing, exposing myself to new thinking and ideas? Ignorance isn't bliss, it's debilitating.

Stephen Covey, the leadership guru, famously talked about the four stages of learning of any skill: 'Unconscious incompetence' – that happy state of total ignorance when you are so incompetent that you don't even realise how incompetent you are; 'Conscious incompetence' – beginning at that depressing moment when the truth dawns and you first become aware of what it is that you don't know and how boxed in you are; 'Conscious competence' – the painful process of struggling to get to grips with what it is that you didn't know. And lastly 'Unconscious competence' – the Eureka moment when you realise that you're now so familiar with what it was that you once didn't know that it's become second nature and you do it quite naturally.

What has dawned on me is that when it comes to developing a church network, Oasis and I have just reached that agonising point of conscious incompetence. 'It's like an exciting nightmare', said one of our trustees last week. He is right, but if we listen to it, this uncomfortable moment is our friend not our enemy – without it we would never recognise our need to grow. As Mark Twain once quipped, 'What really gets me into trouble is not what I don't know, it's what I know for sure but just isn't so.'

if it ain't broke, break it

'Don't act dumb.' That's the one-line response that I got in a meeting where I had just tried to explain why the idea I was putting forward was not quite the 'implausible and impossible dream' it had been dismissed as. 'I'm not *acting* dumb', I protested. 'I *am* dumb. I'm trying to *act* smart. It just isn't working very well.' Everyone laughed, which was a relief. But, if I'm honest, my humour was designed to cover the fact that secretly I thought I was acting a lot smarter than anyone else in the room.

'Give a man a fish and you will feed him for a day. Teach a man to fish and you will feed him for a lifetime.' The truth of that famous Chinese proverb seems undeniable. But as every Change Agent knows, it's not that simple. If you simply teach everyone to fish and leave it at that, all you'll end up doing is slowly depleting the fishing stock, causing a 'Cod war' and then creating long-term poverty. The only sensible and sustainable solution is to think differently – to think interdependence not independence – to revolutionise the fishing, farming,

> Change Agents are driven and creative. They can't stop questioning the way things are.

food distribution and sales industries. Only then will all be guaranteed stable employment and a healthy plate of food each day.

'The human mind', wrote anatomist P. B. Medawar, 'treats a new idea the same way the body treats a strange protein; it rejects it.' That's the problem with being an entrepreneur – it can be very lonely. And sometimes it's not just your idea that gets rejected – you get written off along with it.

Change Agents are driven and creative. They can't stop questioning the way things are. They have the knack of identifying core problems ahead of others and recognising resources where others don't. They constantly exploit new opportunities but most importantly, they fundamentally refuse to give up as they work to persuade entire communities, and even whole societies, to adopt new approaches. They understand Karl Marx's observation: 'The philosophers have only interpreted the world in various ways; the point, however, is to change it.'

An academic may be satisfied when they have expressed an idea. A manager might relax when they have enabled their organisation to meet its budget. But a Change Agent will never rest until he or she has changed the way the world works.

> A Change Agent will never rest until he or she has changed the way the world works.

'Everyone I work with is right behind me – about five miles behind me', I heard someone comment the other day. I smiled because I empathised. But I also recognise that Change Agents are hard to work with. If people are a long way behind me, it's probably because I'm not the best company to walk with. In fact, sometimes I think that I must be the most annoying 'colleague' on the planet – a pain in more than one part of the human anatomy. I often feel like a cultural vandal; I know I'm disruptive, I know I cause chaos. Sometimes even I cringe when I listen to myself in meetings – I can only begin to imagine what it must be like for others.

But here is my dilemma – what else can I do? If, for the sake of an easy life, I go silent on everybody, keep my thoughts to myself, and only regurgitate the party line, what use am I? If I fail to bring what I have to bring, I fail my friends. What's the point of sitting quietly, and then months, or perhaps even years later, when things don't work out, nonchalantly announcing that I knew we were headed into problems all along? Like everyone else, I have a responsibility to bring who I am, and what I see, to the table. I have a duty to do it respectfully and sensitively, but I have a duty to do it all the same. Not to do so would be to abdicate my role rather than fulfil it.

> Being a Change Agent doesn't imply that I'm right – just that I can't keep quiet about the way I see things.

I was raised on the popular doctrine, 'If it ain't broke, don't fix it.' But over the years, I've learnt that this can quickly become the dogma of death, nothing more than a veiled way of protecting the status quo, of letting 'sleeping dogs lie' in the vain hope they'll never wake up and maul you. It's a creed that's content to wait for disaster to loom, if not overwhelm, before responding. Change is only contemplated once failure has already been attained. So I know that unless we nurture a more enterprising and proactive mentality, willing to risk reinventing what is precious to us before it is broken, stagnation and slow demise will be our inevitable fate.

Having said all this, it's important to remember that simply being a Change Agent doesn't imply that I'm right – just that I can't keep quiet about the way I see things. In the words of that great entrepreneur Winston Churchill: 'I won't change my mind, and I can't change the subject.' But to complicate matters even

change agents

further, sometimes the things I think I am most right about turn out to be the things that I am most wrong about. That's why the challenge we face here at Church.co.uk is to build whole churches with a 'can-do' culture. Only then will we succeed in creating congregations where the need for entrepreneurialism is understood and celebrated and, at the same time, Change Agents are held meaningfully to account.

Jesus put all this perfectly in his famous Parable of the Talents. The 'treasure' or 'capital' of the gospel is never honoured when buried in the ground for 'safekeeping'. Shockingly, we discover that it has been entrusted to us to be risked. The enterprising, rather than the cautious, servant is rewarded for his efforts. Or, to put all this another way, sometimes the wisest principle is, 'If it ain't broke, break it.'

an afterword:
tomorrow's change agents

The brutal spectacle of the gladiatorial games was a popular entertainment industry in ancient Rome. Gladiators, normally slaves or political prisoners, were forced to fight to the death cheered on by the bloodthirsty crowds who packed into the Coliseum. But in AD 403 all that was about to change.

Telemachus was a Change Agent. The young monk from what is now modern Turkey, was deeply disturbed by the barbarity of the 'games' and, even more so, by the fact that the Emperor Honorius, who sponsored the contests, claimed to be a Christian, as did tens of thousands of those who regularly took their seats in the audience. But Telemachus was a Change Agent – for him, talking about this evil was not enough. He dreamt of a different world. It was time to stand up and cry, 'Stop.'

The 'little monk', as history remembers him, travelled to Rome, arriving in the capital city during the celebration of the latest military victory over the Goths. The population was in festive mood and a gladiatorial circus was being staged as part of the celebrations. The day after his arrival Telemachus followed the crowds into the Coliseum, and faced with the horror of watching the almost continuous beheading and dismembering, decided that this was his moment for action. Rising from his seat, repeatedly shouting, 'Stop. Stop. In the name of Christ, stop', he began to make his way down, through the crowds, into the central arena.

'Stop. Stop. In the name of Christ, stop'
– Telemachus

At first the crowd thought of the scrawny monk running frantically about the arena, ducking and weaving between the combatants, as a kind of comedy extra. They laughed and applauded his antics. As they began to digest the impact of his words, however, they quickly changed their mood – hissing, booing and bellowing at him at the top of their voices. They began to rain down stones on him to the point where the gladiators joined them by lunging at him with their swords and batons.

When the frenzy was over, the 'little monk' lay dead in the middle of the arena. Slowly the huge crowd fell silent. Then, first as a trickle, growing into a stream and finally a torrent, they began to leave the stadium. It was as though the young monk's last cry was still echoing around the giant arena. Just three days later, the Emperor Honorius issued an edict forbidding all future gladiatorial games.

Scholars still argue over whether Honorius would have bowed to the voice of a single Change Agent, pointing out that we have firm evidence that there was already widespread and growing discontent over the morality of the games that the Emperor could no longer ignore. But all this misses the point. No Change Agent is a lone ranger; they are simply catalysts. As John Pollock, the biographer of William Wilberforce, a Change Agent from another culture and another century, wrote, 'One man can change his times, but he cannot do it alone.' From Telemachus to Mother Teresa, Martin Luther to Martin Luther King Jr., John Wesley to Florence Nightingale, Emiline Pankhurst to Mahatma Ghandi, Lord Shaftesbury to Nelson Mandela, the task of a Change Agent is to articulate a vision of a different future, galvanise popular opinion, overcome the resistance of vested interest, build consensus and offer leadership to others in the journey towards the goal.

The Change Agents of the twenty-first century will be no different. Just like Telemachus and Wilberforce, their task is to act as 'lightening rods' for the transformation they long to see in the church, their local communities and society as a whole; to work to encourage and enable, inspire and persuade their contemporaries to dream of a different world; to believe that 'what is not yet can be' and to not rest until together, with each playing their part, the vision has become reality.

A single snowflake is a fairly insignificant entity – beautiful, unique and romantic, but with no great ability to impact the world. A single snowflake falling on a busy city street is gone within moments. Sometimes, however, when conditions are right, and a snowflake lasts just long enough to be joined by a second, a third, and a fourth, the snow begins to settle. And once the ground is dusted with a layer of fresh snow, as long as the flakes keep on falling, the snow will eventually silence the whole city. Snow has the power to stop traffic.

I have always found Charles Dickens' classic *A Christmas Carol* both inspiring and disturbing. Its central character, Ebeneezer Scrooge, is haunted by three spirits of Christmas. His first encounter, with the 'Ghost of Christmas Past', causes him a measure of sadness as he looks back on events that shaped him into the miserly old killjoy he is. The second spirit, 'The Ghost of Christmas Present', pains him even more, as he is shown the joy that others are feeling at Christmas and discovers something of how he is perceived by his contemporaries. It is the final haunting, however, that brings about the greatest despair and then desire for change in him. 'The Ghost of Christmas Yet to Come' shows Scrooge a vision of a future Christmas in which much of London is celebrating his recent demise. Ebeneezer is terrified by what he sees and asks the ghost, 'Are these the shadows of the things that will be, or are they shadows of things that may be, only?'

'One man can change his times, but he cannot do it alone' – John Pollock

change agents

Upon waking he resolves to live his life in such a way as to forestall the terrible end he saw for himself and invest the years he has left in the community he has spent decades turning his back on. For the first time in his life he understands that not only his tomorrow, but all of our tomorrows, are bound together and shaped by our present activity. Faced with a vision of the consequences of his own inaction, Scrooge decides to become a Change Agent.

In a speech given in Paris in 1910, Theodore Roosevelt noted: 'It is not the critic who counts, not the man who points out how the strong man stumbled, or where the doer of deeds could have done better. The credit belongs to the man who is actually in the arena, whose face is marred by dust and sweat and blood, who strives valiantly, who errs and comes short again and again, who knows the great enthusiasms, the great devotions, and spends himself in a worthy cause, who at best knows achievement and who at the worst if he fails at least fails while daring greatly so that his place shall never be with those cold and timid souls who know neither victory nor defeat.'

Being a Change Agent is not easy. It's not always fun, it's not proof against failure or frustration or fear, and it's certainly not without loneliness and misunderstanding and misrepresentation. But if, as you read these words, your soul is stirred, can you give your life for anything less?

Intelligent Church

A Journey Towards Christ-Centred Community

Steve Chalke with Anthony Watkis

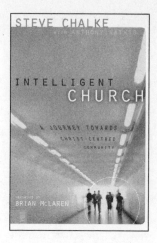

'As St. John of the Cross said: "Mission is putting love where love is not." This book is full of ideas. It should prompt us all to examine the effectiveness of the way local churches are organized.'
— The Most Reverend and Right Honourable Dr. John Sentamu, Archbishop of York

'Everything that Steve Chalke writes is insightful and cutting-edge. Here he argues in favor of a church that thinks and acts in ways that make the Kingdom of God visible and reasonable in a secular society.'
— Tony Campolo, PhD Eastern University, Pennsylvania, USA

The task of the Church is 'to be the irrefutable demonstration and proof of the fact that God is love', claims Steve Chalke. An intelligent church intentionally connects the Bible and its twenty-first-century culture, is authentic and, most importantly, has thought through its practice. In other words, the way it does church is a reflection of its understanding of who God is.

This foundational issue must be addressed by pastors, church and ministry leaders, small group leaders and others as we continue to grapple with the shape of effective church in the postmodern, post-Christian West.

As Chalke unpacks central theological concepts, such as the incarnation, human sinfulness and the Trinity, he points us to the corresponding characteristics of an intelligent church, such as inclusiveness, messiness and diversity. Each thought-provoking chapter concludes with a 'Yes but How?' section, which gives practical suggestions for moving your church along this path.

Softcover: 0-310-24884-1

Pick up a copy today at your favorite bookstore!

The Lost Message of Jesus

Steve Chalke and Alan Mann

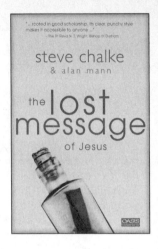

A fresh—and perhaps controversial—look at Jesus by one of Britain's most respected Christian authors.

Who is the real Jesus? Do we remake him in our own image and then wonder why our spirituality is less than life-changing and exciting? Steve Chalke—a high-profile visionary in the United Kingdom and an evangelical recognized not only by Christians but by the general public as well—believes that the real Jesus is deeply challenging. And each new generation must grapple with the question of who he is, because only through a constant study of Jesus are we able to discover God himself.

The Lost Message of Jesus is written to stir thoughtful debate and pose fresh questions that will help create a deeper understanding of Jesus and his message. It is an encounter with the real Jesus of his world—not the Jesus we try to mold to ours. Themes include:

- The Kingdom of God—shalom—is available to everyone now, through Jesus
- The world outside your own church needs to hear of the depth of God's love and suffering
- Jesus was a radical and a revolutionary!
- Jesus offers immediate forgiveness, without cost, to anyone
- Jesus shows us repentance isn't a guilt-laden list of dos and don'ts, but an inspirational vision of a new way to live

Focusing on some of the key episodes, events, and issues of Jesus' life, will see how too often the message we preach today has been influenced more by the culture we live in than the radical, life-changing, world-shaping message Jesus shared two thousand years ago.

Softcover: 0-310-24882-5

Pick up a copy today at your favorite bookstore!

We want to hear from you. Please send your comments about this book to us in care of zreview@zondervan.com. Thank you.

ZONDERVAN.com/
AUTHORTRACKER
follow your favorite authors